# *Live Original*

## HOW THE DUCK COMMANDER TEEN KEEPS IT REAL AND STAYS TRUE TO HER VALUES

## SADIE ROBERTSON

### WITH BETH CLARK

Howard Books
An Imprint of Simon & Schuster, Inc.
New York  Nashville  London  Toronto  Sydney  New Delhi

Howard Books
An Imprint of Simon & Schuster, Inc.
1230 Avenue of the Americas
New York, NY 10020

First Howard Books trade paperback edition July 2015

HOWARD and colophon are trademarks of Simon & Schuster, Inc.

For information about special discounts for bulk purchases, please contact
Simon & Schuster Special Sales at 1-866-506-1949 or business@simonandschuster.com.

The Simon & Schuster Speakers Bureau can bring authors to your live event. For more
information or to book an event, contact the Simon & Schuster Speakers Bureau at
1-866-248-3049 or visit our website at www.simonspeakers.com.

Interior design by Davina Mock-Maniscalco

Manufactured in the United States of America

10  9

The Library of Congress has cataloged the hardcover edition as follows:
Robertson, Sadie.
    Live original / Sadie Robertson ; with Beth Clark. — First Howard Books hardcover edition.
        pages   cm
1. Robertson, Sadie.    2. Television personalities—United States—Biography.    3. Teenage
girls—Conduct of life.    I. Clark, Beth.    II. Title.
    PN1992.4.R5353A3  2014
    070.1'95092—dc23
    [B]                                                                    2014023539

ISBN 978-1-4767-7780-1
ISBN 978-1-4767-7781-8 (pbk)
ISBN 978-1-4767-7782-5 (ebook)

*For my lovely grandmas, who have taught me how to stay true to myself. For my mom, who has called me "original" since I was five and helps me live it. Also for my older cousin Katelyn, whom I have always looked up to and who, as she says, has "put some tools in my toolbox for life."*

# Contents

# CONTENTS

# *Foreword*

When Willie and I started calling Sadie "the Original" back when she was just a cute little girl missing her two front teeth and wearing pigtails, I never dreamed I would be writing the foreword to her book. I knew God had great plans for her because He told me so in His Word, but I had no idea what they would be. We couldn't be more proud of the godly girl she has become and for the ways we've seen her live up to her nickname.

She has done this by listening to God's voice amid all the other voices that are speaking to her and to teenagers just like you— voices that say things like: "If you don't act, dress, and talk like everyone else, you aren't cool." Or "If you aren't skinny and rich, and don't look like a supermodel, you aren't worth anything." Or "If you don't do this, try that, go there, you're a nobody," and on and on.

Living original means being free from all of that. And I can promise you, it's much better on the other side. So come on in, the water's fine! God's voice says nothing can separate you from His love; you are chosen; you are the light of this world; you are a daughter of the King; with Him you can do anything. Doesn't that sound nice? That's what God offers you. That's what comes with living a life that's not like the crowd, a life that's original!

You don't have to have a television show, speak in front of thousands of people, or write a book to live a life that's original. You *do* have to use the gifts that God has given you. God has a great plan for *you* too. What will you do with this life on earth that you have been given? The experiences you have had in your lifetime are unique to you. Good or bad, they are yours, nobody else's. They are your story. You get to choose what you will do with them.

Don't think you are too young to make a difference, and don't tell yourself you'll straighten up your act and start living for God when you get older. God says do it now. He actually says we adults should become more like little children. He says that as young people, you should not let anyone look down on you because you are young, but you should set an example for believers and start now living a life that is worthy of respect. He's talking to you! Young people have unique abilities and energy that we sometimes lose when we are adults.

You can make a difference in your school, in your home, and even in your community. I hope after reading this book you'll have a solid plan for how *you* can live original. It won't always be easy, but I can promise you, it'll be worth it!

—Korie Robertson, Sadie's mom

# Introduction

I've been thinking about the world lately. I know; it's a big subject. So let me narrow it down a bit. When I say "the world," I'm not talking about continents and oceans. I'm talking about everything around us—all the things that influence us every day. I'm talking about what people do and say, what they value, how they live, and what they think is cool or right.

I guess I could try to fit into "the world," but fitting in is not what's most important to me. What's most important to me is living the way God says to live. If the world likes me that way, great, and if the world doesn't, I'm okay with that. I'm going to stick with God and live His way anyway.

The Bible verse that inspires me to live God's way is Romans 12:2:

> Don't copy the behavior and customs of this world,
> but let God transform you into a new person
> by changing the way you think.
> Then you will learn to know God's will for you,
> which is good and pleasing and perfect.

The world and the Bible show two completely different ways to live. The world is full of false advertising. For example, it tells us we can have more fun if we take drugs. It does not say much about the fact that drugs are addictive or that too many can damage people for life or that they can cost them all their money. Even things that are less physically harmful than drugs, like gossiping or cheating, the world seems to think are okay, because "everyone does it." The world says a lot of things are not bad and will not hurt us, when God says they are bad and will hurt us.

A point I want to make now and will make again later in the book is something my parents have told me all my life: God tells us how to live because He wants us to live good, happy lives. He is not into handing out a bunch of rules and then watching us to see if we slip up. The things He tells us to do are designed to help us be the very best we can be and to help us enjoy our lives to the max. God is not a human being, so He doesn't think and act the way people do. He's always loving and forgiving, and He always tries to help us. He's always on our side, and He's always got our back. And in the Bible He tells us to be like Him. It's impossible to totally do that, I know, but if we are trying, then we are going in the right direction.

When the Bible says not to "copy the behavior and customs of this world," it means not to just live like a copy of someone else. It means to live original. I'll write a lot more about how to live original in the last chapter of the book. But for now, I just want to say that living original (which is another way of saying, "Just be yourself—and be great at it") takes courage. It also brings amazing rewards.

Sometimes people try to be original or stand out from everyone else by being different in some way. They might wear crazy clothes or costumes, or put on dramatic makeup or have a hairstyle or hair color that draws attention. I'm all for people expressing themselves in fun ways, but the kind of living original I am talking about is not about that. This book is not about how to make yourself stand out from the crowd just for the sake of standing out.

Living original doesn't mean being different just to be different; it means being a new kind of different—a different based on knowing who you are, knowing who God is, and being confident that He made you in a really cool, unique way. There's no one else on earth like you, and that makes you incredibly special. If you can see how special you are and be strong in it, there is no limit to what you can do and become in life, or to how much you can enjoy it.

> Living original means being a new kind of different and being confident that He made you in a really cool, unique way.

If you will step out and do something good, you might just be amazed at how much people will like and appreciate it. If you are willing to be different in positive ways, you will feel really good about yourself, you will have more confidence, and you can make a difference in a lot of people's lives.

I have been surprised to see that many people really want to do something good in the world but are waiting for someone else to do it first. Just think about it. If you are sitting in class and the teacher asks a question, people are sometimes hesitant to answer, but once one person answers, others start talking too.

I learned this from personal experience at camp one summer. We were having something called Testimony Night, which is an opportunity for people to share what God is doing in their lives. At first, people were pretty shy about it, but then my cousin Reed got up and said some things that were so good they made me cry. When he finished, the youth minister asked me to get up and speak, so I did. Once Reed and I spoke, lots of other people started sharing things with the group. They just needed to see other people do it, and that gave them confidence. We ended up staying there for two hours just listening to people telling their stories.

All the chapters in this book are intended to help you live in a new and different way and to help you find the confidence to live original. In them, I will share some of the lessons I have learned and some I am learning now. I will introduce you to some of the people who have inspired me and made a difference in my life. I'll share some stories about my family and myself and pass along some of the great advice other people have given me about living a good, happy life. I hope the things I have learned will challenge you, inspire you, and make you think about how you want to live.

If you are in a situation where you want to make some different choices so you can live a better life, this book will help you get off to a good start. I'm really glad you're reading it. I hope it will encourage you to be a new kind of different and to live original. After all, that's where you'll find your very best self and your very best life.

*But may the righteous be glad and rejoice before God;*
*may they be happy and joyful.*

—Psalm 68:3, NIV

# CHAPTER ONE

# Think Happy, Be Happy

*I*f there is one thing my family hears a lot, it's this: "Happy, happy, happy." My grandfather Phil Robertson, whom I call "Papaw Phil," is famous for these words, and I am glad he is. I like being part of a family that's happy! I know that not everyone has a happy family, but we can still choose to live a happy life, because happiness starts with what's inside of us, not with what we have or do not have. If we can think happy, we can be happy.

When I was in junior high school, I learned a song called "Garbage in, Garbage Out." I liked it because of the words, and so I played the song for my eighth-grade Bible class and gave a speech about it.

I learned an important lesson from that song: *what you think about will come out in your life.* If you put garbage into your mind, garbage will come out. It's just like what happens if you put junk food into your body. If you eat nothing but chips and desserts, you will not end up being lean and fit and strong. To put it politely, you'll be the opposite. In the same way, if you fill your mind with negative thoughts, bad words, or ideas that are not nice or respectful toward others, you will eventually think bad thoughts, use bad language, and act on bad ideas. The good thing about the "garbage in, garbage out" principle is that it also means that if you fill your mind with positive thoughts, encouraging words, and ideas about how to be kind or how to be a good friend, then all those things will show up in the way you act and eventually become the way you live.

# HAPPY TODAY, HAPPY TOMORROW

There's a connection between the way you think and the way you are. Not only that, there's also a direct link between the way you think today and the person you will become tomorrow. Your thoughts, words, and actions will determine your life more than anything else—more than where you go to college, more than what you major in, and more than the first job you get.

Years ago, someone came up with a great quotation that makes this point really well. I say "years ago" because a version of this saying goes back at least to 1910, and I say "someone" because it has been credited to all kinds of people, from Mahatma Gandhi to Margaret Thatcher's father to the founder of a supermarket chain in Texas.[1] I'm not sure anyone knows who should really get the credit for it, but I like the words, and I know they are true:

> *Watch your thoughts, for they become words.*
> *Watch your words, for they become actions.*
> *Watch your actions, for they become habits.*
> *Watch your habits, for they become your character.*
> *Watch your character, for it becomes your destiny.*[2]

The short "Sadie version" of this quotation is: *your thoughts determine your destiny*. If you want to get a glimpse of where you are headed in the future, start by looking at what you're thinking about today.

Before you go any farther in this book, I want to encourage you to make up your mind to be happy, because your mind is where happiness begins. Thinking happy will not mess up your schedule, and it will not cost any money, but it will be the best investment you can make. It won't even make you tired; in fact, it will probably give you more energy than ever, because happiness just has that effect on people. If you are down or discouraged, decide today to shake that off and become a happier person by thinking happier thoughts. You can make your life and your future better just by thinking happier thoughts.

> Thinking happy will not mess up your schedule, and it will not cost any money, but it will be the best investment you can make.

## HAPPINESS STARTS WITH YOU

Too many people believe that other people will make them happy. This is especially true for teenagers. So many of us think we will be happy if we can just hang out with the "right" group of people or if we can get the boyfriend or girlfriend we want. We also tend to think things will make us happy. We say we will be happy if we can get a certain outfit, pair of boots, new type of phone, or kind of car. We sometimes think we'll be happy if we make the best grades in the class, have the lead in a play, or are starters or high scorers on a sports team.

I have to say to my fellow teenagers: this kind of thinking is just not right. True happiness doesn't depend on a certain group of friends, a boyfriend or girlfriend, a new phone, an outfit, or a car. These things might make us excited for a little while, but they cannot make us truly happy for a long while.

Ultimately, happiness can only come from inside you. If you allow any of these other things to determine your happiness, you will always be let down. The world is not perfect: people disappoint us, friends change or move, parents lose jobs, and bad things happen. Paul said in Philippians 4:12–13:

> *I know what it is to be in need,*
> *and I know what it is to have plenty.*
> *I have learned the secret of being content*
> *in any and every situation, whether well fed or hungry,*
> *whether living in plenty or in want.*
> *I can do everything through him who gives me strength.*[3]

For several years, my family and I have traveled to the Dominican Republic on mission trips. I'll write more about that later, but for now I just want to say that when we go, we meet people who have nothing the world says is important, yet they are happy.

Then I think about the TV show where a couple who won millions of dollars in a lottery was interviewed. This couple said it was the worst thing that had ever happened to them—the money just created a lot of stress. They said their whole family ended up fighting over the money and then lost it because they did not know how to manage it. I'm guessing that these people were not happy with what they had before they won the lottery, so it's not surprising that they weren't happy with more. Happiness is a choice—a choice to be joyful, no matter what the circumstance. This is something adults try to tell us, and I'll admit it: they're right.

The only thing that can really make us happy is a relationship with God. If we know Him and do our best to do what His Word tells us to do, we will enjoy lifelong happiness. He knows exactly what we need in order to be truly happy, and He will lead us to those experiences if we seek Him, trust Him, and obey Him. We have to make a choice to have a relationship with Him. That's the best and most important choice we will ever make. It will not guarantee that we won't have hard times, but it will take us a long way toward a happy life.

As teenagers, there are a lot of things you and I do not have control over. But we are 100 percent in control of the way we think, the way we feel, and the choices we make. We have the power to choose what we think, and what we think will determine the way we feel.

Bible teacher Joyce Meyer says: "Positive thinking doesn't just happen. It's something you have to do on purpose."[4] I always try to put positive things into my mind so that positive things will come out in my words and actions. Like other people, I do not always feel like being positive or happy. Sometimes it would be a lot easier to complain, but what good would that do me? Sure, sometimes it takes more effort to be happy than to be sad, but the result is worth the effort.

> Sometimes it would be a lot easier to complain, but what good would that do me?

We are naturally drawn to people who are positive and happy. When I see a positive person, I think they have their life figured out. They seem to have everything going on. I want to get to know those people because they have something I think is valuable: confidence and a happy, positive attitude. Negative people are no fun to be around and they certainly don't seem confident or together. If we hang out with positive people, their good attitudes will influence us, and we will become upbeat and happy too.

But like Joyce Meyer says, it will not just happen. We have to work on it every day. We have to choose to be positive, even when circumstances are negative. We have to choose to be happy, even when discouraging things come our way. If you are not in the habit of choosing to be happy, it may take some practice. But just keep working on it. You'll get there—and you'll be glad you did.

# THE HAPPIEST PEOPLE I KNOW

When I think about people who are truly happy, I have to mention my two sisters. At the time I'm writing this book, my little sister, Bella, is eleven years old. My older sister, Rebecca, is twenty-five. She came to live with our family in 2005 as an exchange student from Taiwan, and now she is just as much a part of our family as the rest of us.

Bella is only in fifth grade, but I know a lot of fifth graders who already take life very seriously. Bella does not! She loves to laugh and play, and if she is involved in something, she is determined to make it a fun, happy experience for herself and for everyone else. She has a great sense of humor, which I think is very mature for her age. Unlike a lot of kids her age, she does not laugh at bathroom jokes or sarcastic comments about other people. She knows what is genuinely funny in a clean, wholesome way, and she can dish out that kind of humor like no eleven-year-old I have ever met.

I think Bella's main goal in life right now is to put smiles on other people's faces. She just loves to make others happy; that's what she thinks about, so that's how she lives. And if a person's goal is to make others happy, then that person will definitely be happy too.

Another thing Bella does is refuse to get upset over little things. Not long ago, one of her friends was mean to her and blocked her on Instagram. Instead of coming home from school that day pouting about the situation or being dramatic and feeling that no one liked her anymore, Bella simply said, "That was ridiculous. I mean, that was ree-diculous!" She could have easily been hurt or angry, but she was not. In fact, the whole incident really did not faze her. She is not the kind of person who lets other people's actions upset her, and that's a big reason she is so happy.

Rebecca is one of those people who is cute and happy and bubbly almost all the time. She loves to laugh and to make others laugh, and she really enjoys telling jokes. The problem with her jokes is that they may be funny in her native language or in the country where she was raised, but they are not funny at all in English or in Louisiana!

Here's one of her jokes: "One time a banana got hot and took off his coat and slipped." (Yep, that was the joke.) Here's another one: "Once there was a match that had an itchy head; he scratched it and caught himself on fire."

Ha! See what I mean? The fact that the jokes are not funny ends up making Rebecca's attempts at humor kind of funny in their own way. We all laugh at her jokes just because she tries so hard to spread laughter around our family. Rebecca is strong and positive, and other people cannot help but be happy around her. I am so glad she joined our family because just her presence makes me happy.

While I'm thinking about happy people, I can't overlook my

great-uncle Si. Seriously, he is the happiest, funniest, most positive person I know. I'm sure a lot of people my age cannot say they have a strong relationship with their great-uncle, but Uncle Si and I are very close. I like being around him as much as possible, because any time he is involved in anything, it's a guaranteed laugh. He has the ability to make anything fun and to see the humor in things that might be frustrating to other people.

Recently, Uncle Si was duck hunting in very cold weather with Papaw Phil and my uncles. Suddenly, their boat began to sink. I was not there, but I heard the sinking boat brought out everyone's true personality. Papaw Phil took it like a man; he just stood there and watched while the boat sank and then walked very calmly through the water to the duck blind, even though he was about to freeze. My uncles were jumping around screaming, all shouting out different ways to fix the boat. And Uncle Si just laughed and told jokes while he watched the boat go down.

One time something really sad happened to Uncle Si; his house was infested with termites. He and his wife, Christine, had lived in that house for a long time. It was home to them and they really loved it. The termites did a lot of damage to the house before Uncle Si realized it, so he and Christine had no choice but to move out before it fell down.

Uncle Si's response to the situation was not, "Oh, poor me. I'm losing the house I've loved and lived in all these years."

His response was, "Okay. We've got termites. We need to get a new house."

So they moved into a new home, and they are very happy there. I know the reason Uncle Si handled this situation so well is that he does not let his circumstances determine his happiness. He is a happy person, no matter where he lives. He was happy in his old house, and all he had to do when he moved to the new house was take his happiness with him. And for Uncle Si, that was no problem at all!

## WE WERE HAPPY BEFORE . . .

Lots of little girls like the movie *Snow White and the Seven Dwarfs.* I was one of them. One of the songs in the movie is "Whistle While You Work." The lesson of the song is that work—whether it's homework or cleaning your room or a job in some kind of business—does not have to be boring or hard. It can be fun if you think of ways to make it fun. I have never been good at whistling, but I love

> I have never been good at whistling, but I love to sing while I work.

to sing while I work. In fact, I have always turned my study guides into songs or raps to help me remember things.

A lot of people think the job I have now—on *Duck Dynasty*—is really fun. They say they would do anything if they could be a television star. Being on TV is fun at times, but at other times it's hard work—just like anybody else's job. I can choose to be happy about it or to complain about it because I have to film instead of going out with my friends. I almost always decide to be cheerful about it, because that just makes life a whole lot easier than being angry or disappointed.

I guess I learned to be happy when I was very young and worked in my family's duck-call business. This was *way* before most people ever heard of Duck Commander. Serious hunters knew about my papaw Phil's company, but not many other people did. Even though the company was not the big business it is now, it took all of us in the family to make it successful—even me, when I was six or seven years old.

When I was that age, my older brother, John Luke, and I worked for Duck Commander during the summers and at other times when we were not in school. Our cousins Reed and Cole (Jase and Missy's sons) worked with us. The four of us are very close in age. John Luke and Reed were born during the same year. About two years later, Cole and I were born within several months of each other. So all of us have grown up together, and now our two families live right across the street from each other.

When all of us were young, we'd pile into someone's car and make the trip to Mamaw Kay (most people call her "Miss Kay") and Papaw Phil's house, which is about forty-five minutes from our house. In those days, my grandparents ran the Duck Commander business from their home. They had enough land to build a warehouse on their property, so that's where the boys and I went when we "went to work." We packed boxes, answered phones, and did everything else we could to fill orders for duck calls. The song "Hollaback Girl" was popular at that time, and we sang it often, calling it our "warehouse song."

At the end of each day, Mamaw Kay gave us each five dollars. But those payments were not our greatest rewards. Our greatest rewards were all the good times we spent with our grandparents and the lessons we learned from them.

Mamaw Kay and Papaw Phil did not have much money back then, and they definitely were not "famous" like they are today. But they were happy. The boys and I never questioned that. We saw our grandparents work really, really hard to make a small business successful. We saw them love God, love each other, and love our family. We knew from the time we were really young that these things are what make people truly happy.

Mamaw Kay has been a happy person for as long as I can remember. She is the type of grandmother who always has a big hug for her grandchildren, who loves to teach us lessons from the Bible and important things about life, who makes us cookies or our favorite meal for no special reason, and who always sees the best in us. I don't mean she overlooks our faults or lets us get away with being disobedient. She never had any trouble punishing us when we were little (for example, if we argued in her house, we had to go outside until we could be nice to each other), but she is also quick to compliment us when we do well, and she tells us often how much she loves us.

Papaw Phil has also been happy for as long as I can remember. I don't think a lot of people realize this about him because he comes across so differently from Mamaw Kay. He is not one of those sweet, cuddly grandfathers who wraps you up in his arms and starts swinging you around when you go to see him. He's a man who is happy because he is totally comfortable with himself, and he has no need to impress *anybody*. He knows what he believes and he sticks to it, no matter what other people think. He tells the truth exactly as he sees it, and if people don't like it, that does not bother him. I have never seen him sad or shaken; he is solid. And he's happy.

When I think about high school students like me and about all the drama that goes on because someone does not feel accepted by the popular group, I get really sad. Some students spend so much time being upset and disappointed, when they could spend that same amount of time doing what makes them happy and following their dreams—instead of getting upset about what other people think. If we could all just take a lesson from Papaw Phil and accept ourselves even if others reject us, we would be a lot happier. People who can be who they are, and accept themselves as they are, are some of the strongest, happiest people in the world. My papaw Phil is definitely one of them!

All of our family is happy—because our happiness is not based on being on TV or on any of the things that come with it. Not that we never face struggles and not that we never get down about something, but underneath it all, we really are happy. Our happiness is based on loving God and knowing God loves us, and on loving each other. That's what makes us happy, happy, happy.

# *Live Original Challenge*

1. In your own words, why is this true: "If you think happy thoughts, you can live a happy life"?

_____

_____

_____

2. What thoughts are you thinking today that will lead you to the future you want tomorrow?

_____

_____

_____

3. What one thought can you change today in order to make yourself just a little more happy?

_____

_____

_____

4. Take a minute to think about the thoughts you've had today. Do those thoughts make you happy and lead you in a good direction?

_____

_____

_____

## DON'T FORGET

**If you'll think happy, you'll be happy!**

*"Anything is possible if a person believes."*

—Mark 9:23

# CHAPTER TWO

## Dream Big

I'm a dreamer. I guess I was born that way, because I can't remember ever not having a dream. My mom's mother, whom I call Two-Mama, tells me that remembering little quotes and sayings is important. Although I can't remember where I heard it, one of my favorite quotes is: "Dream big and tomorrow make your dreams reality." Thankfully, I have lots of family and friends who not only encourage me to dream big, but who also totally believe in me and are always there to help my dreams come true with God's help.

I believe everything starts with a dream. Every *great* thing definitely starts with a dream. The things that change the world start as little ideas or as little projects, and they become something big. If you do not have a dream, you do not know where you want to go or what you want to do. Without a dream, you miss out on the adventure of trusting God and giving your faith a chance to work. I want to spend the rest of my life giving my faith a chance to work. I want to spend every day dreaming the biggest dreams I can think of and then praying about them and working toward them. I hope that's true for you too.

# MY BIG DREAM

For as long as I can remember, my dreams have had something to do with serving God and helping other people learn about Him. When I was little, my mom used to come into my room every night at bedtime and pray with me. After she left I prayed by myself. My prayer was always the same: I asked God to show me how to spread His Word. I just wanted a chance to tell someone about Him, so every night, that's what I asked God for. I did not realize until years later that this prayer was also a dream.

The older I got, the more the teachers and ministers at my church encouraged my friends and me to share Jesus with other people. That sounded like a great idea, and I had been onto it most of my life, but I had a problem: everyone I had ever met already knew Jesus. Seriously, there was a time when I did not know *anyone* who needed to hear about Him. I couldn't help it; I lived in a small town with lots of churches!

I went all the way through elementary school without ever finding someone who needed to know about Jesus, but I never stopped praying about it or wishing God would answer that prayer. Night after night, I asked God, "Would you please send me *somebody* so I can share about who you are? Just *one* person!" For a long time, that didn't happen.

Finally, when I was fourteen years old, I started filming *Duck Dynasty* with my family, and those episodes first aired when I was fifteen. Because of that television show, I now have opportunities to talk about God every single day—to about a million people. It's crazy when I think about how I get to speak to big audiences or do magazine interviews and now write a book. I can tweet a Bible verse or an encouraging truth about God, and it can go out to people everywhere almost instantly.

For years I could not find anybody to talk to about Jesus. Then all of a sudden, God turned my dream into reality. I can talk to people everywhere because of a TV show. I don't have to look for people to share Jesus with anymore. The way I look at it, our TV show is not an opportunity to put myself in the spotlight; it's a chance for me to put my love for God in the spotlight. Now I can talk about Him to people on the other side of the world from my phone. I love the way God has answered that prayer and made that dream come true for me.

> The way I look at it, our TV show is not an opportunity to put myself in the spotlight; it's a chance for me to put my love for God in the spotlight.

Maybe I'm a dreamer because I come from a family of dreamers. My dad's family and my mom's family both include people who have dreamed big dreams and seen them come true. My parents definitely inherited the "dream gene." In completely different ways, they are both dreamers. They inspire me, and I hope they will inspire you too.

## MY DAD: HE DOESN'T GIVE UP ON A DREAM

My dad is actually the one who took his dad's dream to the next level. Papaw Phil had the vision to make Duck Commander a good duck-call company but not a huge international brand. What happened with my dad and my grandfather was kind of like what happens in a relay in a track meet: one person runs part of the race with a baton and then hands it off to the next person, who keeps on running and takes the baton farther. Papaw Phil was the lead runner. He had the Duck Commander dream, and he started the race; then he handed the company off to my dad, and my dad has taken it farther than Papaw Phil ever thought it would go.

My dad dreamed of growing Duck Commander by getting Papaw Phil's duck calls into more and bigger stores than they were in when he first became CEO of the company. With a lot of effort, he did. You can now find Duck Commander products in places like Bass Pro Shops and Walmart. That's because of my dad. This was not Papaw Phil's dream, but he never tried to talk my dad out of pursuing his dream. Even though he started Duck Commander and it was his dream for many years, once he turned the company over to my dad, he never stood in my dad's way, and he never discouraged him from doing something he thought would be good.

My dad is also the one who had the vision for *Duck Dynasty*. Even though Papaw Phil was part of the *Duck Commander* television show on Outdoor Channel, a show for serious hunters, he didn't think people would be interested in a whole show about our family. He didn't think we were all that interesting and didn't realize that our lives really are different from most. But when someone in the entertainment industry mentioned the concept of *Duck Dynasty* to my dad, he could see it immediately. He knew it was a great idea. He thought it was worth doing, even though he had to work really hard and faced a lot of obstacles trying to make all the arrangements for it. At one point, it was the number one show ever to be on cable television.

I think it's clear that my dad is a visionary, but most people do not have any clue that he is also incredibly hardworking and that he will persevere through any kind of problem. He probably got his persistence from Mamaw Kay and Papaw Phil, because from the time he was really young, he saw Mamaw Kay persevere through rough times just to keep her family fed and to keep the lights on. Later, he saw Papaw Phil stay the course with his duck calls, even when he and Mamaw Kay did not have much money. In those days, Papaw Phil had to travel from one sporting goods store to another in small towns to try to get people to buy his products.

When my dad gets an idea or a project in his mind, he does *not* let it go. He is fully committed to it and works on it until it works. He does not get intimidated if it looks like it might not happen; he just digs in deeper and keeps going for it. When he runs into obstacles, he finds a way to go over them, under them, around them, or through them. When he thinks something is a yes, he refuses to take no for an answer. He might have to work extra hard, he might have to get creative or take a different approach, but *he makes things happen*. He does not stop until they do.

I have learned from my dad that we cannot just have a great idea or a big dream and then drop it when we have a hard time getting it done. We have to believe in it like crazy. If we go after it one way and that does not work, then we have to pursue it another way.

> We cannot just have a great idea or a big dream and then drop it when we have a hard time getting it done. We have to believe in it like crazy.

Whatever your dream is, decide right now that you will not be denied. Don't let haters talk you out of it, and don't let a bad attitude make you give up on it. When someone or something starts telling you no, stand up and shout, "Yes!" If you want your dream to come true, be committed to it, be determined to make it a reality, and don't stop going after it until you see it come true.

## MY MOM: SHE GAVE GOD HER DREAM

When my mom was little, she had the same dream a lot of young girls have. She grew up in a happy, godly family, and she dreamed of having that same kind of family of her own someday. When she married my dad, that dream took a big step toward coming true. When my older brother, John Luke, was born, it took another step, and then it took another one when I came along about two years later.

Although my mom was really happy with our family of four, she also wanted more children. She had always dreamed of having three biological children and adopting another. But when she and my dad decided to add to our family, she did not get pregnant as quickly as she had in the past, so that totally stood in the way of her dream. She did not fall apart or sink into depression over her disappointment; she just prayed a lot and decided to simply wait to see if God would bless her with another baby. She gave God her dream, and she did not get nervous and try to take it back when nothing happened. There was no drama over what she might have felt was the denial of her dream. She just left it with Him.

At that time, we knew a lady in West Monroe who worked with an adoption agency. My mom casually mentioned to her one day that we might be interested in adopting a baby if one needed a home. She told the lady to let us know if something came to her attention, but not to spend a lot of time and energy searching for a baby for us. My mom never tried to force this dream, she just trusted God to unfold it. Mom also knew that adoption could be a very long, complicated process. She had heard all kinds of stories about people who had to wait years for a baby, people who got caught in so much paperwork they could hardly wade through it, and even people who never were able to adopt for one reason or another. So she was very surprised and happy when the lady called her and said her agency had a five-week-old baby boy who needed a family. That baby is now my younger brother, Will. The process of adopting him was amazingly smooth, and I think part of that was my mom's faith and lack of worry. We all thank God for Will, and he has been a blessing to our family ever since.

But there's more to this story. Before my parents considered adoption, they really wanted another biological child. Over time, adoption became a dream for them, just as much as having another biological child was. We definitely believe adoption was God's dream for our family, but God was not finished with our family after Will became a Robertson.

Just a few weeks after Will joined our family, my mom found out she was pregnant. Several months later, my little sister, Bella, was born. Biologically, it would be rare to have two siblings as close in age as Will and Bella are, but that was what God wanted for our family. My mom knew what she wanted, but she cared more about what God wanted. When she gave her dream to Him, He blessed her with more than she ever dreamed of.

Sometimes, we want to hold on to our dreams, but my mom didn't do that. We think we can make them come true if we just work hard enough. Sometimes I wonder if people get a little nervous about giving God their dreams because they are afraid He will not do what they want or that He might forget about them because He is so busy keeping the whole world on track. That's just not true!

I learned from my mom that God really does care about all the things that matter to us. He cares about the really big things and about the little things. Our dreams are important to Him!

God also wants us to trust Him. He is the only one who can see everything about our lives from beginning to end, and He knows just the right time to make our dreams come true and the right time to hold off so He can prepare us for what He has in store. If we will trust Him—even trust Him with our dreams—He will do things so amazing it will blow our minds. Sometimes, we may give one dream to Him and He will make even more dreams come true. When I need to be reminded of that, all I have to do is look at Will and Bella!

# YOU CAN DREAM BIG

Sometimes when I talk to people about dreaming big or about God's blessings, their first response is something like: "Of course you can say that. You're a Robertson. You're on TV. You come from one of the most famous families in America." Those things are true, but being on TV is not what made me dream big. I was dreaming big long before *Duck Dynasty*. When I was just five years old, my mom made a video of me standing on our coffee table talking about how much I loved God and how I wanted everyone to know about Him. Here's what I said:

> We are going to praise Him all our lives. To go up there [pointing to heaven] and we want to stay 'til Jesus comes, and if He comes tomorrow, that's great! We will all go, "Hip hip hooray!"
>
> Hey, we know Jesus and God are up there watching us right now, and they have a huge smile on . . . We love Him, hip hip hooray! Jesus came to earth 'cause He wanted to be nice, and He died for us, for all of us. It doesn't matter if you are a policeman or a jail person. God loves you. Sometimes we make mistakes, but when you make mistakes, that doesn't mean you

are not going up there [pointing to heaven again]. You can still go up there; we know you are worshipping the Lord and loving Him.

And if I was famous, I would still love the Lord. I would not just remember about myself. I would love the Lord.

When you make a mistake you can still go up there 'cause you know if you are worshipping the Lord. We all know that Jesus is in our hearts. He's watching us; he's watching us. He has a big smile on, and it's a huge one and the devil is frowning and that's great! And everybody will be happy. So let's give it up for God!

I was *serious*! But of course I had no idea that years later God would use a television show to make my dream of telling others about Him come true. A television show isn't God's plan for everyone, but whatever He uses is right for each person. His plans fit them as well as television fits me. And let's be real: a television show is hard work and sometimes it is really stressful. I often have to be at work at seven o'clock in the morning and work until very late at night. And I'm a high school student. When I miss school in order to film, I have to make up my work, and I have to do the same amount of homework as everyone else in my class. I also play sports, so I have to go to practice and show up for games. Like other people my age, I love hanging out with my friends, but I can't always do that because sometimes I have to work or travel because of the show.

So being on TV is not all glamorous; parts of it are just plain hard work. It can complicate my schoolwork and my social activities just as much as having a job at the mall complicates those things for other people. Sometimes after basketball practice, I am really tired and I just want to grab something to eat without being recognized. But then someone does recognize me, takes a picture of me looking not my best after practice, and posts it on the Internet. (I am thinking, *Would you want* your *picture on the Internet after you have been practicing basketball for two hours and you are exhausted? Me neither!*) Being a TV star gives me some opportunities that others do not have, but it does not make me better than anyone else, and it does not make my dreams more likely to come true. All of us need to dream big, pray big, work hard, and trust God to bring our dreams to pass.

> All of us need to dream big, pray big, work hard, and trust God to bring our dreams to pass.

I mentioned at the beginning of this chapter that for as long as I can remember, I prayed and dreamed about serving God. Now, when I have an opportunity to share God's Word or tell someone about Him, my mind races back to when I was five years old and I prayed for God to please give me just one person to talk to about Him. Every time I get to share about Him, I remember those prayers, and that makes me incredibly grateful for the platform God has given me because of my family and our TV show.

I want to share with you one of my favorite "dreaming" scriptures from the Bible:

> *This is the confidence we have in approaching God:*
> *that if we ask anything according to his will,*
> *he hears us.*
> *And if we know that he hears us—*
> *whatever we ask—*
> *we know that we have what we asked of him.*
> —1 John 5:14–15, NIV

This scripture really assures us that God hears us and that we can have complete confidence in Him. But it tells us another thing too: our dreams need to be "according to his will." So whatever you dream, make sure it lines up with the kind of life God wants us to live.

With that said, I want to encourage you to dream *big*. It does not matter whether or not a lot of people know about you. For a long time, I was just a praying little girl in a small town in Louisiana. I did not know how God was going to make my dream come true and answer my prayers, but I did know I had to trust Him with it. Now, of course, I have more dreams, and I am trusting God with those too.

When you dream, don't just think about a few things you might like to do someday if they work out. Get a real dream. Make it a big dream. Make it something you could never do by yourself, something that will stretch your faith, a dream that will give God a chance to do something huge for you.

# *Live Original Challenge*

*1.* What's the biggest dream for yourself you can think of?

_____

_____

_____

_____

*2.* What small step can you take toward your dream today?

_____

_____

_____

*3.* Think about whether your dream is according to God's will. If it is, write out a commitment today to never give up on your dream.

_____

_____

_____

*4.* Take a minute to pray to God and give Him your dream and wait on Him to make it come true.

_____

_____

_____

_____

## DON'T FORGET

**Dream big and allow God to make your dreams reality!**

*We can rejoice, too, when we run into problems and trials,*
*for we know that they help us develop endurance.*
*And endurance develops strength of character,*
*and character strengthens our confident hope of salvation.*

—Romans 5:3–4

## CHAPTER THREE

# Never Give Up

Have you noticed how many people give up on things? I'm kind of amazed when I hear about athletes who do not stick with a team for an entire season or students who drop classes because they are too hard or people who give up on their brothers or sisters when those siblings go through a hard time. I mean, really, giving up is not something to be proud of. It might make things easier for a little while, but it does not make anyone a stronger person.

I'm interested in becoming a stronger person. To do that, I know I will have to persevere through situations that might tempt me to give up. But I know God will give me the grace and courage I need to deal with things that are hard, and let's face it: life does get hard sometimes. The world is full of haters and disappointments and mistakes, but we do not have to let these things keep us from going after our dreams or from reaching our potential. Sometimes people say or do mean things to us, and sometimes circumstances just don't go our way, but we have to push those things aside and keep moving forward.

Several men in my family have taught me a lot about perseverance and about never giving up. I want to share their stories with you, and then I'd like to tell a story about a man I never met but who inspires me anyway. But first I want to tell you about a day that made me want to give up, a day I had to decide whether I would quit or whether I would rise up and fight. This was not the only rough day I've ever had; it's just the one I want to tell you about right now.

I know you have hard days and hard situations too. I know there are times when it seems like everyone is against you and you are the only one who is for you. I hope this chapter will inspire you to keep going against all odds and to never give up until you reach your goals.

# I SURVIVED SURVIVOR DAY

Every year, there is one day that I absolutely love and that all my friends dread worse than having their wisdom teeth taken out. It's called Survivor Day, and it takes place at a Christian camp in Louisiana, not far from where I live. It's a camp my great-grandfather started in 1967 and a place all my family loves. We've made lots of incredible memories there, and in fact, my parents first met there when they were in the third grade—and Mom's parents met there years earlier. People keep asking me if I am going to carry on the family tradition and marry someone I meet at camp. Who knows? That will be another story for another time.

Survivor Day works like this: we never know when it's going to happen, but when it does, it is *intense*. For several years, one of my secret wishes has been to participate in the television show *Survivor*, but so far I haven't been invited, so Survivor Day at camp is as close as I can get. Most people moan and groan when the staff surprises us with Survivor Day, but I'm thinking, *Bring it on*. It's a very hard day physically and mentally, but when it's over, we always discover that the whole experience has been designed to teach us a powerful spiritual lesson.

A couple of years ago, Survivor Day happened on the very first day of camp. Now, *that* was a shock to everybody. We were all sleeping peacefully in our wooden cabins, having sweet dreams in our bunks, when suddenly someone burst into our room at about four o'clock in the morning, screaming, "You better run! You better run! It's Survivor Day!" We had to get up very quickly and start running as fast as we could.

> We never know when Survivor Day is going to happen, but when it does, it is *intense*.

We all met at a central place in the middle of camp and divided into teams of about ten people each, which is what we always do. We had to come up with a team name, design a flag, and wear the team bandanas that were given to us. My team's bandana that year was orange—and I'm not a big fan of orange. I already had a bad feeling about that day.

Each team chose a leader, and my team decided to make the most athletic person in our group the leader. There were a couple of football players and big, strong guys on our team, but the guys didn't want to lead, so they chose me. I am pretty athletic, and I am good at sports and games, but I am not as athletic as a football player, and some of our contests required brute strength. I decided to rise to the challenge of being the leader because the group seemed to want me and because I was also the person who had been going to camp longer than everyone else. So I felt some responsibility to lead the others.

On Survivor Day, we have to do all kinds of really hard, seriously grueling things, and the team leader usually ends up doing the hardest things of all. We can't eat until we win a snack or a meal in one of the contests. My team was trying so hard that day, but we were not winning, so we were really hungry, and I ended up passing out. At that point, I wanted to quit and just go take a shower and a nap. I found myself thinking, *This is only a bunch of games, and my team is losing, so why should I keep wearing myself out?*

Let me just give a little background here. No matter where I go, if Two-Mama is around when I leave the house (and she's around a lot), she always tells me, "Be a good example and a good leader." In my mind at that moment, I could hear her saying those words to me, and I knew she was right. I could not just say I was tired and give up. Everybody was exhausted. They needed a leader who would rise up, not one who folded under the pressure. I had to round up all my energy and have a positive attitude so I could help everyone on my team finish well, with their best effort, even if we were not going to win. So I didn't go take a shower and a nap. I got back in the game and encouraged my teammates to give the rest of the competition everything they could give it.

After a completely exhausting day, I finally got to go to our campfire at about ten thirty that night. At last, I could relax! At least that's what I thought. But I was wrong. We had one more challenge—and on top of that, I and my team had not eaten anything all day.

For the last challenge, each team leader had to carry each teammate—one at a time, from one place to another—running all over the camp. Most of my teammates could not help because they were blindfolded or had their legs tied together or something. The staff made them helpless on purpose, so they would have to depend on the leaders to get them where they needed to go. Even if I had been able to easily find my team members and if they had all been close together, this would have been really hard. But it was super-hard because they were spread out *all over* the camp, and I had to run up and down hills and do a lot of backtracking to get all of them across a big field to our home base. This had not been an easy day: I had worked hard all day long, I had passed out, and I had helped keep my team's spirits up. I did not want to run around and carry people long distances. I just wanted to stop and walk—all by myself, without being responsible for people who could not do anything to help me carry them.

I learned so much that day about the importance of not giving up. Even though my team did not win the contest, we had the satisfaction of knowing we had given it our best. We refused to let other teams walk all over us without a fight. We did not win a prize, but we came away with our self-respect.

> Only real champions and people of character and strength keep going past the point of wanting to give up.

One of the biggest lessons I learned that day is that anybody can quit; people quit all the time, and no one thinks very highly of them for doing it. Only real champions and people of character and strength keep going past the point of wanting to give up. Only real champions cross the finish line when they are completely worn out. But that's where the rewards are.

## PAPAW HOWARD: NEVER GIVE UP ON SOMEONE YOU LOVE

I can't write a chapter about never giving up without including a story about my mamaw and papaw Howard. Their first names were Alton and Jean, and they are my great-grandparents on my mom's side of the family. They lived across the street from me, so I remember them very well, even though Papaw died when I was seven years old and Mamaw died when I was sixteen.

Mamaw and Papaw Howard were both spiritual giants and great people. Everyone at our church loved and respected them. My papaw was a successful businessman who owned a jewelry store, a chain of discount stores, warehouse clubs, and a publishing company. I will write about these things later in the book, but they are not what made him great. He was also a man of great vision in the church and started several ministries that are still helping many people today. But that's not what made him great either. What made him great was his love for Mamaw, whom he called "Queenie."

Here's part of their story. My papaw had been to war, and when he returned he fell in love with and married a beautiful young lady. A week after my grandfather, their first child, was born, my papaw was getting ready for work when heard the baby crying. He rushed into the kitchen to find my mamaw staring into space. He spoke to her, but she did not respond. Papaw had no choice but to take her to the hospital. After hours of crying and praying, my papaw heard the sad news that his sweet young wife had had a nervous breakdown. That started the journey that he and my mamaw traveled together for more than sixty years.

Not many medications were available to help Mamaw in those early years, so my papaw dedicated himself to helping her live as good a life as she could. Even though he was very visible in the community and at church, he was never embarrassed or ashamed of Mamaw. He loved her so much. He never hesitated to invite missionaries, dignitaries, or all of our big family to their home for meals, where he would fry fish and Mamaw would cut up potatoes for French fries.

As the years went on, better medication became available, and Mamaw's quality of life improved. It seemed like a miracle. But that's not the miracle. Here's the miracle. "Jean Howard" is the name hundreds of people would say if asked to name a prayer warrior or woman of great faith. Papaw also wrote one time that Mamaw was "a Martha and Mary all wrapped up in one."

Mamaw could practically quote the entire Bible. One of her favorite verses was Isaiah 41:10, in the old King James Version:

> *Fear thou not; for I am with thee:*
> *be not dismayed; for I am thy God:*
> *I will strengthen thee; yea, I will help thee,*
> *yea, I will uphold thee with the right hand of my righteousness.*

I can still hear her saying those words with great emphasis.

Papaw would later write that he could see how God welded their bond of love and how there were now thirty-nine of us who came from their great love. Almost all of us worship at the same church each Sunday.

As Mamaw and Papaw got older, Papaw's health declined first. After he cared for Mamaw for so many years, the time came for Mamaw to take care of Papaw, and she did so with grace and love. She read him scriptures and cooked his favorite meals.

Their love was an awesome example of never giving up, even when your dreams have no hope of being realized. Papaw stood by Mamaw through some very dark days, and in doing so left our family a legacy of steadfastness and commitment that I will always appreciate and remember.

# PAPAW PHIL: HE STARTED SMALL—AND KEPT ON GOING

When Papaw Phil was in college at Louisiana Tech, he was a great football player. He was so great that when he decided to leave the football team because it took too much time away from duck hunting, a guy named Terry Bradshaw took his place. Terry Bradshaw became a Super Bowl–winning quarterback, and now he is on TV talking about football. He's so famous that he even does things like commercials for weight-loss products. I'm just saying that to make the point that Papaw Phil was really good, and if he had stuck with his football, who knows? Maybe he would have won the Super Bowl and would be in weight-loss commercials today.

But football was not Papaw Phil's passion. His passion was duck hunting. That was probably the last thing he thought about every night and the first thing he thought about every morning. What he really wanted to do with his life was to hunt and be really good at it. But I'm sure he wondered how he would ever support his family if he did get really good at it.

Papaw Phil had a gift for knowing what ducks are supposed to sound like and figuring out how to build duck calls to make those sounds. So he started dreaming about being able to support his family selling the duck calls he made. He started with just one kind of duck call, and he worked on it and improved it over the years. Then he made another kind and another.

There's a reason people call Papaw Phil "the Duck Commander." He spent a lot of years learning everything he could about ducks. He knows how they fly and what their habits are. He knows the differences between diving ducks and perching ducks and dabbling ducks. He knows which ducks have good meat to eat and which ones don't. But most of all, he knows about duck sounds, because every type of duck makes a different sound, and males make different sounds than females. His ear is amazing. It's a gift not many people have, and he used it to make his dream come true by making the most accurate duck calls on the market.

He did not make the perfect duck call on his first try. He made one after another after another, tweaking and refining every one until he got it just right. He never allowed himself to get frustrated with a duck call that was not perfect just because he had spent a lot of time working on it. If it was not exactly right, he just kept fixing it or started over. Making those first great duck calls took a lot of patience and perseverance.

For Papaw Phil, being able to support his family by selling duck calls did not happen fast, and our whole family had to work in the business in order to make it successful, but it did happen. He reached a point where he was able to provide for his family—and he's in pretty good shape today because of those duck calls!

What I've learned from Papaw Phil about never giving up is that there is nothing wrong with starting small if you just keep going. You just take what you have, whether it's a *little* idea or a *little* bit of extra time or a *little* bit of money, and you make the most of it. You do the best you can with that little bit, and you keep working at it, and pretty soon it will grow. It might even get so big that the whole world knows about it someday.

There's a Bible verse that talks about this. Zechariah 4:10 says:

> *Do not despise these small beginnings,*
> *for the Lord rejoices to see the work begin.*

If God tells us not to look down on small beginnings, then we can feel excited about the little things in our hearts. If God can love the seed of a dream or an idea that seems minor or random, you and I can love those small beginnings too. If God gets happy just seeing somebody begin to work on something, you and I can also be happy about taking a first little step toward our dreams and about taking more little steps after that first one.

> If God can love the seed of a dream or an idea, you and I can love those small beginnings too.

Maybe you have a dream today, and something inside of you is telling you it will work out someday if you just don't quit. Maybe it's something really specific, like Papaw Phil and his duck call. Maybe it's something you don't think you could ever make any money doing. I'm sure people thought that about Papaw Phil. Maybe it's something you know you will have to work really, really hard to accomplish. The truth is, most dreams are like that. If they are dreams worth having, they are worth working hard to achieve.

No matter what your dream is, go for it. Don't think you can't start working on it just because it seems small right now. Do what you can with your small dream, and it will eventually become your big dream.

# DON'T TAKE NO FOR AN ANSWER

One of my great-grandfathers on my mom's side was named Luther Neal Shackelford. Our family called him Papaw Shack, but most people called him Luke—this is where John Luke got his name. Well, Papaw Shack had a father who was an alcoholic. His mother eventually left his dad to support and raise her seven children who were still living at home. Their life was not an easy one, but my papaw and his siblings made the best of a bad situation by staying in school and playing sports. My papaw's dream was to play college basketball. That dream gave him a purpose and goal in life. After high school, my papaw, like his older brothers, knew the only way he would go to college was to go on a GI Bill. So he did. He and all five of his brothers joined different branches of the armed forces and served our country during wartime.

Papaw Shack joined the Marine Corps in 1948, just before the Korean War. He was the only man in his barracks who could type, so he was designated "clerk typist" after finishing boot camp. Papaw claimed that God made sure he could type so he would be spared the front lines of war. He laughingly said that if he was sent to the front, he could strangle the enemy with a typewriter ribbon.

When people realized Papaw was an athlete, he was allowed to join the base sports teams. He played on these basketball teams for the five years he was stationed stateside, in California. Each base had teams that competed against other bases, colleges, and Amateur Athletic Union teams. These base teams were highly respected, and Papaw was honored to continue playing the game he loved to play.

This arrangement lasted the five years Papaw was stateside, but then he was sent to Hawaii and Japan. There, Papaw found himself in a tent camp in freezing weather and extremely rough conditions. He thought his basketball dream was over. But he soon heard that the base was forming a team to entertain the troops, so he set out to find out how he could play. When he asked his commanding officer about trying out, the officer told him no because all the players on the team had to have played in college. Papaw hadn't gone to college yet, but he didn't take that no as a final answer. He found out where the team was practicing and went to watch. God once again intervened in Papaw's life when Papaw discovered that the coach of the team was a former coach of his. That coach immediately requested that Papaw be assigned to the team. He even got to play against the Harlem Globetrotters!

When Papaw did get to go to college, he wasn't able to realize his dream of playing college basketball, even though he was accepted as a "walk-on" at Oklahoma State University under the famed coach Hank Iba. He already had a growing family and schoolwork to think about, so he chose to give up college basketball for his family. But he did get to play for the United States Marine Corps for six years, and he valued his assignment to that team so much.

Papaw left a family legacy of basketball. I am now the fourth generation of basketball players in our family, and my coach is my uncle Jeremy Luther Shackelford, Papaw's youngest son, who did get to play college basketball. Most important, Papaw left us with a strong sense of what makes life valuable—and that is family. When he was a child, he didn't have the kind of family life that many dream about, but he made sure his children had that life. And his children passed that love on to their children, and now I am blessed to have the family I love surround me with constant support. It's not unusual for me to have as many as twenty family members watching one of my games. I love looking up in the stands and seeing their smiling faces, knowing it all started with my papaw Shack, who didn't take no for an answer when he had the dream of basketball in his heart. You may not have a big family like I have, but you can have a big dream, and if you never give up, you'll be amazed at what God can do.

# THE MONOPOLY MAN

If you are like me, you have probably played the game Monopoly. But do you know the story behind the game? Someone told it to me, and I want to pass it along to you.

In 1929, America was in a very bad situation because the stock market had crashed and people hardly had any money. A man named Charles Darrow could not find a regular job, so he took every little odd job he could find to support his family. One day, he sat down and invented a game with play money. He made the game so people could pretend to buy and sell real estate—something most people could not even dream of during those days.

He started the game by drawing on his kitchen tablecloth, then he improved it by using little pieces of material or scraps he found, then improved it again by building and painting its pieces. Family and friends soon came to his house to play the game, and it became very popular because it gave people without much money a chance to dream of being involved in high finance.

Eventually, Darrow was able to sell his board game, starting at four dollars each. Then he tried to sell it to the Parker Brothers game company, who turned him down because they counted fifty-two things that were wrong with the game—fifty-two reasons they thought their customers would not want to play it. But Darrow did not give up. He went on to manufacture the game himself. Later, Parker Brothers had a new president who found out about the game and offered to manufacture it and give royalties to Charles Darrow. Those royalties made him the first game inventor to ever become a millionaire.[5]

# *Live Original Challenge*

1. What's the hardest thing you have ever done or the hardest day you have ever lived? How did you get through it?

_____

_____

_____

2. Is there someone in your life whom you shouldn't give up on? How can you continue to love that person?

_____

_____

_____

3. What small steps have you started taking toward your passion or your dream? Are you determined to keep going and not give up, no matter what?

_____

_____

_____

4. Why do you think it's important to never give up?

_____

_____

_____

## DON'T FORGET

**Anybody can quit.
Only a real champion and a person of character and strength
can keep going and refuse to give up.**

*Do not throw away this confident trust in the Lord.*
*Remember the great reward it brings you!*

—Hebrews 10:35

# CHAPTER FOUR

# Confidence Is Key

Have you ever met someone who is really smart or talented, but they act like they don't know it or like they don't believe in themselves? They walk around looking at the ground. They slump and slouch, they mumble, and they avoid other people. Often, the biggest problem these people have is that they lack confidence. They may be great students, athletes, or musicians, but if they do not have confidence, they don't become everything they can be and they don't inspire anyone else. Instead, they just go through life being above average in some areas, but not truly great.

In this book, I try to offer a lot of encouragement about ways to live original and ways to live a good, happy life. Confidence is the key to actually being able to *do* all of these things. It's the difference between "average" and "great." I believe you can be great. It's not always easy, but if you can develop a strong sense of confidence, you will take a huge step toward greatness.

A former football player named Joe Namath says, "When you have confidence, you can have a lot of fun. And when you have fun, you can do amazing things."[6] I have not ever met Joe Namath, and I don't really know anything about him. But I like what he says about confidence, and I totally agree with him. I hope this chapter will encourage you to become a confident person so you can do amazing things with your life and have fun!

# SHE HAD CONFIDENCE

One of my all-time favorite movies is *The Sound of Music*. I just love it. When I was in the fifth grade, in our middle school choir program, I sang a solo of one of the songs Maria sang in the movie. Ever since then, it has been "my" song and it's a happy, upbeat tune called "I Have Confidence."

In the song, Maria is on her way to the Von Trapp family's home for the first time. She knows she will work as the governess (like a nanny) for seven children, and she knows their father is a military man. But there is a lot she doesn't know about her new job, so she is excited and scared at the same time. She also has questions and doubts about whether or not she will be good at being a governess.

As the song goes on, Maria moves from being worried to figuring out what she will do to teach the children and to earn their respect. By the end of the song, she has a plan based on simply showing them she has confidence in herself. She knows that they will never respect her if she does not respect herself, so she decides to find in her heart the courage and confidence she needs. The song is like Maria's personal pep talk. She starts with admitting that she is intimidated by her new job, but by the end, she is ready for it.

I love the way Maria sings "I Have Confidence" because it shows us that reaching a point where we can really be confident does not always happen quickly. To get to that place, we sometimes have to face our fears, think through what we need to do, tell ourselves to just get courageous, and take a step of faith—then believe it will work out well. That's the way Maria found her confidence, and that's how you and I find ours too.

# CONFIDENCE TAKES TIME

In many ways, I was confident when I was little. In the video that shows my five-year-old self standing on the coffee table talking like a little preacher, I said, "If I become famous someday, I will not just remember about myself. I will remember God. Let's give it up for G-o-d!" But when I was young, my confidence was like a roller coaster; sometimes it was high and sometimes it was low. I figured out at one point that if I let another person's words or actions affect my confidence, I really was not confident at all. At that time, I did not know how to hold on to the confidence I did have and keep it strong, but I eventually learned. Now when something happens that might cause me to lose my confidence, I can see the dip coming: I know my confidence is about to sink. Maybe someone says something rude to me, or maybe I make a big mistake or don't perform as well as I would like at school, in sports, or at my job. As soon as I recognize the temptation to lose my confidence, I have to fight against it.

Defending my confidence is kind of like defending my team's goal in a basketball game. I play a lot of basketball, and unlike football, it's a sport in which every player has to play both offense and defense. When it's my turn to be a defender, I work hard to make sure the other team does not score. I try not to foul, of course, but

I try to get in their way or force them out of bounds so they cannot be successful against me.

In the same way, I don't want anything that would steal my confidence to be successful against me either. Most of the time, preventing a dip in confidence is not about physical or athletic skill; it's about a battle I fight in my mind, with my thoughts. If someone says something about me that I know is not true, I just tell myself what is true. If I make a mistake or feel like I have failed at something, I tell myself I had a bad day or was not as prepared as I needed to be—but I will do better next time. I have a sign in my room that says, IT'S NEVER TOO LATE TO START THE DAY OVER. I love that sign because it reminds me that even if I mess up, I can start over right now and do better next time. No matter what happens, I remind myself that God created me, He loves me, He is with me, and He is on my side. All those things are true for you too. And if you believe them, they will make a big difference in your life.

> If someone says something about me that I know is not true, I just tell myself what is true.

## A GUARANTEED CONFIDENCE BUILDER

When I was in eighth grade, I had to make a decision about whether I was going to be confident or not. A girl started picking on me for some reason. This was about the time *Duck Dynasty* first started, so maybe she was jealous of that. I'm not sure, but I definitely got a little hate from her.

During that time, I felt more insecure than ever before, and I started getting quieter—a little reluctant to speak up or stand up for myself with the kind of strength I'd had in the past. I knew that the Bible talks a lot about standing up for what's right—and sometimes that means standing up for ourselves. The only way to be bold and stand up is to have confidence. I talked to my mom about this. She always seems confident and does not seem to worry about what other people think. My mom told me she dealt with girls who were mean to her when she was in junior high school too, just like most girls do, and that it was not really about me.

Sometimes we get in our own little world and think, *I'm the only one going through this*. That's why I think it's important for girls to know that almost everyone goes through something like this in her life. If something like this is happening to you, you are not alone and it really is not about you. When people say or do mean things, it's not because you have something wrong with you; it's because the other person is struggling with their own insecurities. My mom reminded me of this and helped me to see that maybe this girl was going through some tough things in her life and projecting them onto me. She also told me that all I could control was how I acted and how I let the girl's words and actions affect me. She encouraged me to be as kind as possible in return, but at the same time she helped me to be strong and told me that speaking up for myself when necessary was okay, just to do it with love.

Mom turned out to be right. Later, this girl and I sat down for a heart-to-heart talk, and she shared with me some tough things she was going through in her life and apologized for the way she had treated me. I was proud that this girl trusted me enough to share these things with me. I knew the only reason she was able to trust me was that I had worked hard on myself, trying not to let the things she said or did hurt me and striving to remain kind to her despite the way she treated me. This was not always easy, but I knew it was what God was asking of me. I was rewarded with her actually apologizing—something I never thought would happen.

During that situation, I quickly saw that I needed a major dose of confidence, and I knew exactly where to get it. I had a whiteboard in my room. On it, I wrote the Bible verse that is at the beginning of this chapter: "Do not throw away this confident trust in the Lord. Remember the great reward it brings you!" (Hebrews 10:35). I read that verse over and over, every single day, for a year.

At that time in my life, I had several opportunities to speak in front of groups, and I was always really nervous about doing it. One of the prayers I prayed most was, "God, give me confidence." Because I had gotten the truth of Hebrews 10:35 into my heart and mind, I knew I would be rewarded when I became confident through Him. For me, becoming confident took a lot of praying and a lot of focusing on what God's Word means for me personally, but it worked. Now I totally stand up for myself—and that girl from eighth grade doesn't bother me anymore!

My best suggestion for anyone who wants to become a more confident person is this: find some Bible verses that relate to you and go over them and over them until you are actually living them. In most countries of the world, it's easy to get a Bible or to find one online. If you have this book in your hands, you can also probably get a Bible if you don't already have one. You can even Google "scriptures on confidence" and come up with a good place to start. Finding out what God thinks about you and what He says about your life is one of the most important things you can ever do, and the place to learn those things is in His Word. The Bible has been the biggest source of the confidence I have developed, and I believe that if you read the verses you choose for yourself and get them into your brain and your belief system, they will do the same for you.

# NEW EXPERIENCES IN NEW YORK

The things I have mentioned in this chapter helped build confidence in me. Little by little, they gave me the courage I needed for experiences I never dreamed I would have. One goal I have had for myself for a long time and try to encourage others to also aim for is *consistent* confidence. Real confidence does not come and go. Real confidence is inside you, and it stays with you no matter what you go through.

> Real confidence does not come and go. Real confidence is inside you, and it stays with you no matter what you go through.

In September 2013 I needed a consistent level of confidence more than ever before. I was invited to something called Fashion Week in New York City. To explain it simply, Fashion Week is a time when fashion designers show everyone their new designs. Everywhere you look, you see media people, makeup artists, hairstylists, design assistants, and designers. And you see models—*lots* of models.

I know a lot of teenage girls would think being part of Fashion Week would be the greatest thing ever, but when I first arrived, I saw that it could be very intimidating. Let me explain.

When I showed up for my first appointment, I walked into a room full of models from places like Russia and other European countries. To me, they all looked about six feet tall and were super skinny. They were pretty obsessed with their weight, so instead of having snacks or treats, they smoked cigarettes and drank coffee. They all seemed to be a lot older than I was, or at least a lot more experienced. They were quiet, and they seemed either sad or kind of angry. No one in the room was in a very good mood.

I totally stood out when I first saw all of them. There I was, a cheerful sixteen-year-old from Louisiana, eating M&M's and saying, "Hey, y'all!"

Many of them did not say a single word back to me. They just looked at me like they had icicles in their eyes. Without using words, they sent me a strong message: "What are *you* doing here?" It was pretty uncomfortable!

But I knew I was there for a reason. It was where God wanted me to be that week. The fact that I even got invited was kind of a miracle. I was there to showcase my line of "Daddy-approved prom dresses." Those kinds of dresses are not very popular with professional models.

As I went through the week, I realized something. A lot of girls my age would think those models might be some of the happiest, most confident people on earth because the fashion industry views them as the most beautiful people in the world. But most of them did not seem confident at all. They seemed to be trying to live up to an image someone else had created for them—to be people they were not—and that is not good for anyone. They actually seemed to have a lot of insecurities, and that comes from having the wrong idea about what confidence is and where to get it. They seemed to be looking for it in places it does not exist, seeking it from their looks or their professional connections. They cared way too much about their outward appearance—and confidence is an inside thing. It has nothing to do with how people dress or what they look like. If people try to become confident by trying to make themselves look better or feel better, they will never get there.

By the end of Fashion Week, some of the models I met really warmed up. One time, I got my hair and makeup done before any of them did, and they were very curious about that. One even asked me, "Why do *you* get to go first?"

I explained to them that I had to do media interviews, which is not something many models do. I was able to talk a little bit about *Duck Dynasty*, which is not a big deal in the models' home countries, so they had never heard of it and had no idea what I was doing or why I was doing it. As they started to understand more about me, some of them thought what I was doing was awesome. A few even said they wished they could do something similar. Others seemed to look down on me and be frustrated because I got to get my hair and makeup done before everyone else. What I went through with the models, especially in the beginning of Fashion Week, could have caused my confidence to take a major dive. I could have totally lost it over the comments people made and the icy looks they gave me. But I didn't. God had been training me all of my life—with a special emphasis during my eighth-grade year—to be strong and confident in who I am in Him.

One Bible passage that really applies to my time at Fashion Week is 1 Peter 3:3–4:

> *Don't be concerned about the outward beauty of fancy hairstyles,*
> *expensive jewelry, or beautiful clothes.*
> *You should clothe yourselves instead with the beauty*
> *that comes from within, the unfading beauty*
> *of a gentle and quiet spirit, which is so precious to God.*

The way to become confident is through a relationship with God. In my life, I know that the stronger I get in my faith, the more confident I become as a person. That's the way it works. Just give it a try and you'll see.

# Live Original Challenge

1. What would you do differently in your life if you had as much confidence as you would like?

_____

_____

_____

2. What kinds of situations can cause you to lose your confidence? What Bible verses can you use to strengthen yourself when these things happen?

_____

_____

_____

3. What are your best qualities? Knowing your strengths and good qualities helps you grow in confidence.

_____

_____

_____

4. What is one dream or goal you would like to achieve, and how will confidence help you get there?

_____

_____

_____

## DON'T FORGET

**No matter what you want to do, confidence is key!**

*The temptations in your life are no different*
*from what others experience.*
*And God is faithful.*
*He will not allow the temptation to be more than*
*you can stand.*

—1 Corinthians 10:13

# CHAPTER FIVE

# You Can Only Fix You

My dad told us about a time he was on an airplane and the person sitting next to him took literally hundreds of selfies with her phone. That's all she did the entire flight. Now, I must admit, I have taken a selfie or two in my life, but Dad said she was taking them the entire flight, and when she wasn't taking a selfie, she was looking through and editing her album of selfies on her phone. I thought maybe she was taking off on a big adventure she had been excited about for a long time and wanted to post pictures of herself finally on the plane, headed for someplace exotic. That would have been kind of understandable. Or I thought maybe she was going to Snapchat someone, but then I realized she would not have had any service in the air. My mom even asked my dad if maybe the girl recognized him and was trying to fake him out by appearing to take selfies but getting a few photos of him along the way.

We will never know what she was doing or where she was going that day, but my dad insisted that she really seemed to be simply snapping selfies like crazy—seriously, *tons* of them—then editing each one to make it look better than the real photo actually did. This is *not* what I mean when I talk about "fixing yourself"!

When I say, "You can only fix you," I mean that each of us is responsible for ourselves. This is something people my age really need to understand. Blaming our parents or friends when we do things that are not good for us is easy. Making excuses is easy, and as teenagers, we can come up with some *really* good ones. Taking responsibility is not so easy, but it's what helps us grow up. One way to think about taking responsibility is to look at it as the opposite of blaming other people. Something that really gets on my nerves is when people blame others for problems they created for themselves or for things that may not be anyone's fault; they just happened. I don't know about you, but I *know* when something is my fault. I might not want to admit it, but I know it. I also know that if I try to blame someone else, I will not grow (plus, I would be lying if I said it was someone else's fault when it wasn't). But if I take responsibility for whatever happened and look to see what I can learn from the situation, I will grow because of it.

> One way to think about taking responsibility is to look at it as the opposite of blaming other people.

# GROW UP GREAT

I want to grow up to be a great person who makes a positive difference in the world. I hope you do too, because you have all the potential you need in order to do that. If we are going to make that happen, we have to start taking responsibility for ourselves now, while we're young. We have to learn to be good at who we are.

If we want to be good at sports, we have to go to practice; we have to stay in shape; we have to build our endurance. We also have to discipline ourselves to take responsibility for doing the things that are necessary for being good athletes. The same is true for musicians, people who want to excel in schoolwork, and anyone who wants to do anything well. I once heard that it takes ten thousand hours to be an expert at anything. It's not just about talent, it's about hard work and putting in the practice and the hours to make yourself great at anything you want to be great at.

If we want to be our very best selves, we have to try to do what's right and be the type of person other people want to be around. We need to be kind and positive and make good choices. Sometimes we have to work at being kind to others. For some people that takes a little more work than it does for others. Or you may tend to see the negative in others, to see the glass as half-empty. Being positive may be something you have to really work on or practice. Two-Mama tells me that my uncle, her son, seemed to have been born negative. She says that when he was a little boy, she would make him tell her three positive things about his school day as soon as he walked in the door, before he could say anything else. She did this to try to teach him to think more positively. Sometimes positivity takes practice.

Also, some people are just not that easy to be kind to. That's when we have to remember, "You can only fix you." You cannot control what other people say or do or how they act. You can only control how you act in response to them. Jesus said the greatest command is love: loving God with all your heart and loving your neighbor as yourself (see Matthew 22:37–39). Being kind, positive, patient, generous, not jealous, not rude, unselfish—all those things the Bible defines as love—takes work. And only you can work on those things for yourself.

"Fixing you" means that whenever we notice a character flaw, we fix it. When we are tempted to do something wrong, we stand strong against it. We make decisions we are proud of—decisions that build us up on the inside and that benefit not just ourselves but others. And we don't make decisions that will lead to disappointment or cause us to live at a level that is less than we want for ourselves or God wants for us.

All of us are growing and becoming what we are supposed to be. We aren't there yet. If we want to reach a place of being our very best, we have to start now to fix ourselves and make adjustments in our lives. I can only fix me, and you can only fix you. If we will all do that, we can make the world a better place.

# I CAN'T FIX ANYBODY ELSE

I mentioned in chapter 1 that whatever you put into your mind will come out. When people make bad choices about what they watch, read, or listen to, the garbage they put into their lives reveals itself in their decisions, their choice of friends, or the ways they spend their time. And almost always, it comes out of their mouths.

One time I was with my friends and one girl started using really bad language. In Louisiana, we call that "cussing"! She did not use just one or two bad words; she let a whole string of them go. I was totally shocked!

Most people hear the kind of words she used from time to time. A lot of people use them when they stub their toe, but it's a whole different deal when someone hammers them all the way through a conversation. That language does not make her a bad person, but it puts hateful speech in my mind, and God wants my thoughts and words to be pure and joyful.

After I got over my initial shock, but before the girl had said too much, I told her, "When you're with me, I don't want to hear that stuff. Your words affect the people around you, and I don't like the effect they could have on me." Maybe she thought I was being picky, but I had learned the "garbage in, garbage out" principle when I was in junior high school and I had not forgotten it. I did not want the words she chose to use to get into my mind or come out of my mouth the next day. So I told her what I thought.

Whether or not the girl continued to speak the way she did was her choice. If she was okay with doing that in her life, that was her deal. I could not stop her, but I did not have to listen to her. When people speak that way, it influences the people around them. When it affects me—or you—I have a right to stand up for myself and to decide what I will or will not listen to and allow into my brain.

My point is that I could not do anything about the way that girl spoke. She was in charge of her own vocabulary! I could not do one single thing to improve her choice of words, but I could do everything about whether or not I chose to listen. I am learning that we can't change other people, but we can always change ourselves. In 1 Timothy 4:12, the Bible says,

> Don't let anyone think less of you because you are young.
> Be an example to all believers in what you say,
> in the way you live, in your love,
> your faith, and your purity.

My job is to obey God's Word, and that often means being different from the people in the world around me. God says I need to speak in a way that sets an example for others. That's what I'm determined to do, and I hope you are too.

# A GREAT EXAMPLE OF FIXING YOURSELF

When people see my mamaw Kay on *Duck Dynasty*, they have no idea what a strong person she is, how hard she has worked all of her life, or how much she has been through. They do not know she has faith like a rock and that if she believes in something and starts praying about it, she will not let it go until she gets her answer. But she doesn't just pray; she gets busy doing everything she can to fix her problem. She does not sit around and wait on God to do everything for her; she does all she can to help herself.

> Mamaw Kay does not sit around and wait on God to do everything for her; she does all she can to help herself.

Mamaw Kay has always been this way, I guess. She has definitely been like this for as long as I have known her. I have heard enough to know there was a time in her life when she could not fix anything or anyone who really mattered to her. All she could do was take responsibility for herself and work hard to make her life better. Here's the story.

For as far back as she can remember, Mamaw Kay dreamed about having a "pioneer man" for a husband, a happy marriage, and a loving family. But her life did not turn out that way, at least not at first. Early in their marriage, Papaw Phil was definitely a pioneer man, but he was also really wild and he did not treat Mamaw Kay well. I'm not talking about a little partying for a little while; I'm talking about some things that really hurt Mamaw Kay and made her life *really* hard for ten years. She could not do anything about him or his choices; she had to take responsibility and do what she could to make it through a very hard time and to grow in the middle of it.

No matter how bad things got, even when Papaw Phil was not around, Mamaw Kay kept herself and her boys (my uncles Alan and Jase, and my dad) going. She did not let her troubles steal her dream or keep her down. One time, she even worked at a chicken place just to make enough money to pay her rent and utilities. With every job she had, she was a dependable hard worker, and she kept learning new skills so she could get better jobs.

Mamaw Kay's grandmother, who would have been my great-great-grandmother, told her one time, "You have to fight for your marriage." Mamaw Kay never forgot that. The harder things got with Papaw Phil, the harder she fought and the more she took responsibility for herself and her boys. She could have let herself have all kinds of problems and blamed Papaw Phil for them. I think a lot of people did blame him, but she did not. I won't go into detail about this story because Mamaw Kay does that in the book *The Women of Duck Commander*, where she writes a lot about what she had to do to survive during that time. She worked hard to keep her dream alive when everyone around her told her to give it up. She owned her decision to marry Papaw Phil and did everything she could do to help herself, while she prayed for God to help her too.

For years, Mamaw Kay kept that dream in her heart all alone, with no one to encourage her or help her very much. She had to help herself. She was the only person who believed Papaw Phil could change, and when he did, he changed *totally*. Now Mamaw Kay does have the strong, happy, loving family she always wanted—and people all over the world tell her they wish they had a family like hers. Her dream took years to come true, but she fought for it and prayed for it until it happened.

If I ever find myself in a problem I think is someone else's fault and feel tempted to blame them, all I have to do is think about Mamaw Kay. I remember that she refused to blame Papaw Phil even for problems he did create; she just found ways to do what *she* needed to do to get through them. Getting to her dream was not easy, and it took a lot of years and a lot of effort, but she got there. She says the relationships she has now with Papaw Phil and her family have been worth everything she went through, and she has taught me through her example that I cannot control what other people do, but I can control the way I respond.

## HOW TO BECOME YOUR BEST YOU

It's one thing to tell ourselves, "I can only fix myself." It's another thing to know how to do that. I have a few suggestions.

Don't be obsessed with yourself; take responsibility for yourself. I'm kind of shocked sometimes when I see how obsessed people can be with themselves—for example, that girl who was sitting next to my dad on the airplane. She's not alone, though. Lots of people think about themselves more than they think about others. Some are so focused on how great they are or are so worried about what others are thinking of them that they forget other people are great too, and they forget to put others first. Being obsessed with ourselves is not the same as taking responsibility for ourselves.

When we decide to take responsibility for ourselves, we can definitely acknowledge our good points, but we also have to look at areas where we need to grow and improve. Then we have to do something about those things. For example, do you have trouble being on time? That's really disrespectful toward others, so maybe you can work on not being late anymore. Or do you sometimes tell little lies in order to keep from getting in trouble? That's compromising your integrity, so you could decide today that you are going to tell the truth, even if you have to go through some consequences.

The whole idea of personal responsibility is not always popular, but as I said earlier, it's one of the best ways we can grow and become mature. Think of it like a workout for what's inside of you. Taking responsibility may feel heavy or hard—like lifting weights sometimes does—but it makes the muscles of who you are and makes your character strong.

> Taking responsibility makes the muscles of who you are and makes your character strong.

Get great friends. If you are anything like I am, your friends are really important to you. I have a great group of close friends. Some of them are in my grade at school, others are a year or two older. So obviously, what makes us friends is not that we are the same age, but that we share the same values. All of us love God, and we want to live our lives the way He teaches us in His Word. This makes everything about being a teenager so much easier for me.

No one can choose their family, but all of us can choose our friends. Whether you have a great family or a family you think is not so great, you can still choose awesome friends. They may not be the most popular group, but if they are people who love God, live by His Word, and have strong character, you can't go wrong.

Smart adults will tell you that you become like the people you hang around. One of the facts of life is that the people we are around have a major influence on us. So spend your time with great friends, and they will help you become great too.

Find a wise grown-up. I hope you have smart, wise grown-ups you can trust in your life, but I realize that not everyone does. I do have great parents, grandparents, aunts, and uncles, but sometimes I meet people or get messages from people who say they cannot count on the adults in their family to help them grow up strong and godly. My best advice is to find a teacher, a coach, a neighbor, or even a friend's family member who will help you learn to take responsibility for yourself and to make good choices.

Sometimes teenagers feel that all grown-ups do is correct us or that all they want to do is keep us from having fun. That's not usually true. Some grown-ups have already done the things we think would be "fun" and found out that those things are not fun at all. Sometimes those things got them in big trouble! Usually, when grown-ups try to correct us or tell us what to do, they are trying to keep us from making the same mistakes they made because they want us to have an easier journey through life than they did.

So if you do not have a parent or grandparent to help guide you, find someone else. Look for someone who has had a lot of experience in life, because that's how people become wise. Look for someone who is kind and patient and someone you think can help you get where you need to go in life. I'm pretty sure, if you'll look, you'll be surprised at the adults who would really love to be part of your life.

Put good things into your brain. I wrote about this earlier in the book, but it's so important that I want to mention it again. One of the best ways to take responsibility for yourself and for who you will become is to be disciplined about what goes into your mind.

One time, a friend of mine put some nasty things on Twitter and I unfollowed her immediately. She got upset about that and I told her, "If you want to change what you post, I will follow you again." I knew that if I let myself read the words she tweeted, they would get into my head and would influence my thoughts and what came out of my mouth. In that situation, I could not change what she posted, but I could fix me.

The same thing is true about the shows we watch on TV and the music we listen to. I hear people complain a lot because they think there's nothing good to watch on TV. When they say this, I think, *The only way you can know it's not good is if you watch it. If it's not good, why are you watching it?* Our family believes *Duck Dynasty* has brought a positive message to television. That's at least one good show people can watch!

My point is bigger than *Duck Dynasty*, though. I'm trying to say that one way we can take responsibility for ourselves is to fix what goes into our heads. We can be disciplined about what we watch, read, and listen to and about whom we follow on social media. People say that "what's out there" is so destructive to the world—all the sex and violence and bad language—but I say what's destroying the world *around* you does not have to destroy *your* own world. You can be bigger than that!

Sometimes we have to make unpopular decisions like the ones I just described. Other people may not like them, but we do not make them for other people. We make them for our own good.

# *Live Original Challenge*

*1.* Why do you think taking personal responsibility and fixing yourself is important?

_____

_____

_____

*2.* What's the biggest thing you think you need to fix about yourself right now? How can you start?

_____

_____

_____

*3.* Is there someone in your life who is causing you trouble? Instead of blaming that person, how can you respond to the situation in a way that will help you grow?

_____

_____

*4.* Do you need to work on yourself by changing your group of friends? Who are some people who could influence you in positive ways and how can you develop relationships with them?

_____

_____

_____

## DON'T FORGET

**You can't change anyone else.
You can only fix you!**

*In the same way, let your good deeds shine out for all to see,
so that everyone will praise your heavenly Father.*

—Matthew 5:16

## CHAPTER SIX

# Let Your Smile Change the World

One of my favorite quotes is: "Don't let the world change your smile, let your smile change the world." It's credited as "anonymous," so I don't know who wrote it, but I think that person was very smart. The words remind me to bring joy to the world. Even when I am not having a good day, if I will just smile, I'll bring a little joy to myself and to the people around me. That's a good thing to do. I can do it, and so can you.

This quote also encourages me to be genuine everywhere I go. It talks about *your* smile, not someone else's smile. I don't ever have to pretend to be someone I'm not just to impress other people or to fit in with a certain group. I only need to be myself. Some people will like who I am, some will not. So I will hang around with the ones who do. My mom says: "You can please all of the people some of the time, some of the people all of the time, but you won't ever please all of the people all of the time." So don't let that get you down. Don't let people you can never please change your smile.

What's true for me is true for you. You do not have to try to impress anyone either. God made you in a unique way so you would have something great to offer the world around you. If you let the world shape you and influence you—instead of influencing it—you will miss the chance to share with others what God has given you.

Your smile represents everything about you. One reason I like the quote "Let your smile change the world" is that I think the world needs to be changed in a lot of ways. It needs to become a happier, more positive place. I know those changes can start with something as simple as a smile and then, as we begin to believe we can have an impact on the world, we will build the courage to do bigger and bigger things.

> Your smile represents everything about you.

# LITTLE BY LITTLE

Someone once asked me what changing the world means to me. I have always thought of it as something that happens one step at a time, by one person at a time. No one changes the world overnight or all alone. But if we all do what we can do, eventually it happens. Things become different.

Sometimes people think they cannot do anything to change the world. They think they're nobodies, or they decide they do not have the brains, the experience, the skills, the money, or the creativity to make a difference. But that's just not true. Everybody can do something. If that something does not seem like very much, that's okay; do it anyway. I remember when I wanted so much to share Jesus with someone and I could not find anyone who needed to know about Him. So I prayed and asked God to give me opportunities. He did.

If you don't think you can do anything to make a difference, start praying. Pray that God will give you the chance you need. Especially if you are a Christian, ask God for a way to share His love with someone. If you can tell one person about the hope of Jesus and they tell another person, eventually you can bring a lot of change. Not everyone will believe what you say about Him. Not everyone will take it well. But if you can help one person change and that one can help someone else, you can make a huge impact. Just do what you can do, even if it seems very small—because it might just turn into something really big.

# JUST BE YOURSELF

Years before *Duck Dynasty* started, some people in my family had a television show called *Duck Commander.* It was on a small hunting network for serious outdoorsmen. It did not have the kind of ratings *Duck Dynasty* has had, but it was a full television production, complete with a crew and everything.

Let me explain something about filming. When people are wearing microphones in order to film a show, the guys who do the sound can hear everything said, even casual conversations. When you are filming a TV show, you tend to forget you have on a microphone. If you need to go to the bathroom and forget to turn off your mic, they can even hear you peeing. Embarrassing.

After being around my family for a while, one of the men who worked on the sound noticed that our family did not use bad language or trash other people; we spoke with kindness and honesty. So he decided to really pay attention to everything we said to see if we would slip up. We never did, and that was very surprising to him.

One day he told Papaw Phil that he had been listening to see if we would use cuss words or talk behind someone's back. He also told Papaw Phil he never heard anything bad or mean-spirited come out of our mouths, and asked why.

Instead of giving him a quick answer, Papaw Phil said, "Do you have a few hours?"

Papaw Phil took the man to his house and spent the afternoon explaining a relationship with God to him, and the man became a Christian.

A lot of people come to Jesus because of what they *do* hear—maybe a Bible verse or a great story about something God has done in someone's life. This man came to Christ because of what he did *not* hear—negativity, trash talk, complaining, or bad language. The Robertson men on the show were just being themselves. Because they were genuine, that man's life was changed forever. That's one way to change the world.

You may not have a television show or a sound guy who can listen to every word you say, but you have people around you at school, in your neighborhood, or in your family. Just be yourself and be genuine around them. You never know what a big difference that could make.

My dad came home one night with another great example of this. The president of a very large, successful company came to meet with Duck Commander about doing some business together. Some of the Duck Commander employees took this guy to lunch and they prayed before the meal, not thinking anything about it. Praying before meals is normal for us, but it was shocking to this guy.

This man is not a Christian. He later told my dad that he didn't even know what it means to pray, but he could not stop thinking about it. He said he had never seen people do that at a business lunch, and it had been on his mind ever since. He shared the story with others and couldn't stop talking about it or thinking about it.

The morning after the meeting at Duck Commander, he got up and felt the need to pray. But he did not know how; he didn't have any idea what words to say. He told my dad that he got down on his knees and no words came out of his mouth, and then he just started crying. We are talking about a big powerful man—on his knees crying and then telling my dad about it. It's amazing what God can do with just a little thing like praying before a meal!

The man then asked my dad to help him learn more about God, and now my dad is e-mailing him Bible verses to study so he can learn about God for himself. His life will be changed because of this. Remember this story next time you think there is nothing you can do to change the world. A simple prayer at the beginning of a meal is changing this man's world and the world of those around him. Who knows how far-reaching this simple act will be?

## LET'S MAKE THE WORLD HAPPIER

The world needs to change for lots of reasons. Just to name two of them—too many people are hungry and too many children are orphaned. Another reason the world needs to change is that it's just so negative! That might not sound like as big of a crisis as world hunger or some of the other things that are happening, but it is still a problem. When I say "negative," I mean the world has become discouraging, not encouraging; it's often full of anger, not peace; there are tons of hate and not nearly enough love.

One reason the world has become so negative is social media. When my mom and dad were my age, social media had not even been invented. Even now, my papaw Phil acts like it doesn't exist! He knows about it, but he does not get involved in it. I am pretty sure our lives would be much easier if we didn't have so many ways to post anything and everything for the whole world to see.

Parents and other adults talk a lot about how bad social media is, how hurtful it can be to people, and how they sometimes wish we did not have access to it. I have to agree with them. From my perspective, there are some horrible things on it, and some people use it to be really mean and offensive to others. Sometimes people let a tweet or a post on some site ruin their entire day, and I want to ask, "Why are you reading that stuff? Why don't you choose to read something good?"

If I could say anything to grown-ups who are so upset about the things that happen on social media, I would say this: Everyone gets to choose who they follow, who they interact with, what they post, and what they read. A lot of the things you do not like can be blocked. If you are unhappy about social media's influence on the young people around you, you can change your world and theirs by setting some standards for what they can and cannot look at.

Even though I can see the problems with social media, I also see a lot of good in it. In fact, I think we can use it to make a huge difference in the world if we make just a little effort. I have about one million followers on Twitter, and I do my best to use Twitter for good. I try to post encouraging messages, and I only follow people who also want to use social media in positive ways.

I get a lot of messages from fans, and I do not reply to or follow most of those people. But one day, I had an unusual opportunity with someone who tweeted me from Florida. This girl tweeted Cole first, then me. We did not respond. Then she tweeted me again with this: "I was wondering if you could help me change and be a better person."

Most teenagers would not put something like that on social media because they would be embarrassed, so I could tell this girl really wanted answers, and I decided to direct-message with her. Our conversation went something like this:

**ME:** "What do you want to know?"

**GIRL IN FLORIDA:** "Whoa, you noticed me."

I then told her what I would do if I wanted to become a better person. I would start with the fruit of the Spirit (Galatians 5:22–23) and use that list as my instructions. It says that when the Holy Spirit of God lives in us, we will become people of love, joy, peace, patience, kindness, goodness, faithfulness, gentleness, and self-control. Pretty good list.

**I WENT ON TO ASK HER:** "Are you involved in a church?"

**GIRL IN FLORIDA:** "No. And I don't have any friends who go to church."

**ME:** "Do you know what the gospel is?"

**GIRL IN FLORIDA:** "No."

In a series of messages, I wrote to her: "God sent His Son, Jesus, to this earth through a virgin named Mary. That's the hope we have. We don't fear death because we know God has a perfect place He is preparing for us right now. To repent is to give all your sins to God and all your life to God. It's like becoming a brand-new you."

> I hope you will commit to only posting words and pictures that make people happy, not angry or hurt.

For me, sharing the gospel is the best possible way to use social media. If I can do it, you can do it too. I hope you will join me in refusing to look at negative, discouraging, disrespectful things on social media. I also hope you will commit to only posting words and pictures that make people happy, not angry or hurt. If enough of us come together and do this, we can change the world.

# NOW HERE'S A MAN WHO CHANGED THE WORLD

In chapter 3 I talked about my great-grandfather, Two-Papa's father, whom I called Papaw Howard. But I want to share more about him here. He was one of the most amazing world changers I have ever heard of, and I am glad I had a chance to know him before he passed away. He truly believed he could change the world, and he did.

First of all, and most important, he was a man who loved God more than anything or anybody else. In 1967, he founded a Christian camp, called Camp Ch-Yo-Ca (a name that comes from the first two letters of the three words "Christian Youth Camp"). This camp is an amazing place where lots of teenagers have come to know Christ or grown in their relationship with Him, and I wrote about it in chapter 3. I am sure our family may never know how many lives have been changed or how many great ways people have made a difference in the world as a result of something that happened to them at that camp.

Papaw Howard was also a very smart entrepreneur. One of his first businesses was a jewelry store he started with his brother. He and his brother also went on to start a chain of discount stores—this was before "discount stores" were popular in almost every city and town in America, so he was definitely ahead of his time. He later started a warehouse club chain with my grandfather, which they sold to Walmart and is now called Sam's Club. He also started a publishing company. He wrote a lot of songs that are still sung today, and he put together several hymnals. The most popular hymnal was called *Songs of Faith and Praise*; that hymnal has sold more than three million copies. I am amazed when I hear about people who know about that hymnal. It's everywhere, even in the most random places.

In addition to those things, he was a real estate developer; he also owned several restaurants and clothing stores. He was involved in the oil and gas industry, and on top of that he started a traveling singing group and had a music company.

Papaw Howard wanted people everywhere to know about Jesus, so he started a ministry with others in our church and called it World Radio. His dream was to put on radio programs all over the world, so people could hear the gospel preached even if there were no preachers in their area. The ministry still exists, spreading the love of God in native languages in over one hundred countries around the world.

My great-grandfather really cared about people. He did a lot to help people in our community, and in fact, Mamaw Kay got a job at Howard Brothers Discount Stores when things were so hard for her and Papaw Phil. I do not know whether or not he knew what a hard time she was having, but she has always appreciated the opportunity to work for him.

Papaw Howard's love for people went beyond our hometown. He also founded a relief ministry to help people during natural disasters. As part of the work of this organization, Two-Papa drove a truck across Europe twice to deliver food to people in Poland when that country was under martial law in 1981–82. This organization provided relief on 9/11, when the World Trade Center was attacked, and after Hurricane Katrina, which hit our home state of Louisiana hard, as well as in many, many other places.

Every year at Christmastime, the kids in our family love to sing a funny old song with him. It's called "Ticklish Reuben" and it tells the story of a guy who thinks everything tickles him. The chorus has lots of "ha-ha-ha"s in it, and when Papaw Howard got to that part of the song, he always ended up laughing so hard, and all of us laughed with him.

Talk about someone who made a difference! And people tell me he got a lot of ideas while he was fishing. Maybe more people need to spend time fishing if they want to think of ways to change the world.

# SMILES THAT SPREAD HOPE

In 2013, our family and friends had a great experience when we got to meet the Daraja Children's Choir of Africa. They are an amazing group of twenty-four young people who love God and spread hope and joy everywhere they go. They came to visit us in early July and stayed at Camp Ch-Yo-Ca for a few days and sang for our church. Then we had a big Fourth of July celebration in our backyard with these precious kids. We ate and played together, and they sang for us. Their smiles and awesome hugs were contagious; they seem to be the happiest people on earth.

While they were here, we were able to talk to the adults who were taking care of them while they traveled America singing and spreading God's light, and they told us some of these children's stories. Many of the children had lost either one or both of their parents. Two of the children's parents died of AIDS while the choir was visiting America. And every single one of them lived on less in a year than we receive in a week here in America. Yet they were smiling!

Seeing their faith and love as they sang songs to God, such as "How Great Is Our God" and "We Worship You," and thinking about the true meaning behind the words was life changing. These kids had faith that God is greater than all their problems, and you could see that faith in their smiles. Even though I had never met them before, their smiles changed my world!

> These kids had faith that God is greater than all their problems, and you could see that faith in their smiles.

## A SMILE THAT CHANGED MY WORLD

After the success of *Duck Dynasty*, our family started hosting groups from the Make-A-Wish Foundation. This organization tries to make wishes come true for sick children and teenagers, and a lot of them wish for a trip to Duck Commander and a chance to meet our family. I love that we do this, and I always look forward to days when people from Make-A-Wish come to visit. We always do our best to make their time with us special, and we pray with them before they leave. Our time with them is very emotional; there's usually not a dry eye in the room! We pray for them because we care about them, and we are really honored that they want to spend time with us.

Seeing people who have cancer yet are happy in the midst of it has really changed me. It makes me want to be happy too and not get upset over the problems I have. The world would say healthy people are definitely better off than sick people, but I have been amazed to see how much joy these patients have because of what they have learned about God in what they have been through.

A lot of the people from Make-A-Wish stand out in my mind, but I want to write about one specific boy, who was about fourteen years old. He came to Duck Commander with his parents and sister. He did not say much, but he had a big smile on his face, and I could tell he was happy. He seemed so excited to be in our company headquarters, to watch us film part of a *Duck Dynasty* episode, and to take pictures with us. I talked with his mom for a long time, and she told me how hard his journey has been for their family but how much closer they have become because of it. She also shared that everyone in their family had become better people as they watched him overcome the obstacles of his illness.

People with a worldly point of view might think what happened to this boy would be the worst thing they could imagine. But he and his family chose to put God right in the very middle of it, and they knew the only way to get through this hard time was with Him. That one boy's smile changed my world. When I realized what faith and courage were behind his smile, it made me want to be a better person. When our visit with him and his family was over, all I could think was, *If he can be joyful, I can too*. And so can you.

# Live Original Challenge

1. How can you change the world in some little way, starting today?

_____

_____

_____

2. Will you commit to reading and posting only positive, encouraging messages on social media? What changes will you need to make to keep this commitment?

_____

_____

_____

3. Who inspires you to change the world, like my papaw Howard inspires me? How can you take the lessons you have learned from that person and make a difference?

_____

_____

_____

4. If you could change the world in one big way, what would you do? When can you start?

_____

_____

_____

## DON'T FORGET

**You and your smile can change the world!**

*"For even the Son of Man came not to be served but to serve others and to give his life as a ransom for many."*

—Mark 10:45

## CHAPTER SEVEN

# ARK:
## Acts of Random Kindness

If you saw the movie *Evan Almighty*, maybe you remember this conversation between God and Evan.

> **GOD ASKS:** "How do you change the world?"
>
> **EVAN ANSWERS:** "One single act of random kindness at a time," while he writes on the ground with a stick. He writes the letters A-R-K, to stand for "**A**cts of **R**andom **K**indness."

One reason I like this part of the movie is that it does not just talk about being kind; it talks about being kind in random ways. The way my friends and I use the word "random" is to describe something that is not planned or thought out, maybe something totally unpredictable or something that feels like it came out of the blue. When I think of acts of random kindness, I know I don't have to spend a lot of time thinking about them; I can just do them on the spur of the moment, when I see an opportunity.

This is important because it shows people that others do think of them and care about them—and it reminds them that there are still good people in the world. In fact, acts of random kindness surprise people in really nice ways. And most people really enjoy happy surprises. Some even go on to do something nice for someone else because acts of random kindness are contagious. One leads to another, and that leads to another, and pretty soon a whole cycle of kindness is happening.

> Acts of random kindness surprise people in really nice ways.

I also like the scene where Evan writes "A-R-K" in the dirt because it teaches me that people do not have to do huge things that attract a lot of attention in order to change the world. Something like sending someone a text with a scripture or a little reminder such as "God loves you!" can make a person's day. Or randomly paying for the order of the car behind you at drive-through restaurants or coffee shops can spread joy. As I wrote in the previous chapter, sometimes just a smile can change the world. And sometimes simply being kind can do it. Just ask Evan!

# OH, YEAH—THE JEEP

My boyfriend is really great at doing acts of random kindness. He is the type of person who picks up people on the side of road and will do whatever he can do to help, even if it is not wise. He has the kind of heart that is always eager to be good to others—even if he has to go out of his way or sacrifice his time or money—and that's something I really like about him.

One time when he was driving me to the airport in his Jeep, we saw some people who appeared to be out of gas on the side of the road. They looked very worried. We stopped to ask them what was wrong.

They had a child in their car and told us they were trying to take him to the hospital. They did not ask us for money; they simply asked if we would use the Jeep to push their car to the nearest gas station, which was pretty far away. Without stopping to think about the damage this could do to the front of the Jeep, my boyfriend said yes.

We had no way of knowing whether the people were telling us the truth or not. Maybe they were; maybe they weren't. But either way, we did what we could to help them. When we arrived at the gas station, the father thanked us and basically said, "There need to be more people like you in the world." Maybe he will remember what we did for him and start looking for ways to do something similar for someone else.

Something important to know about acts of kindness: while they are definitely about the person you do them for, they are also about you. What I mean is that even though you can't control how other people respond to them, you can decide whether or not you do them. I hope you will do them, because being kind makes you feel happy. Most of the time, it makes others happy too. But if it does not, at least you have done something you can feel good about.

If you set a goal to make someone's day every day, I think you will be surprised at how much better your days—and your life— will be. By choosing to help others and make them smile, you will end up being the one with the biggest smile. Giving really is better than getting.

We need to be willing to look past ourselves and see what we can do for others. This is part of being a kind person. Even when it is not convenient—and even if it might mess up the car!

## KINDNESS IS A FRUIT

When I wrote the story of the girl who wanted advice on being a better person, I mentioned the fruit of the Spirit (Galatians 5:22–23). When you receive Jesus and His love in your heart, then you receive the fruit of the Spirit. Kindness is one of those fruits; it's on the list right after love, joy, peace, and patience. This tells me that being kind is *really* important, and it's something God enables us to do when He lives in us.

If we know God, the fruit of the Spirit will show up in our thoughts and actions all the time, but we have to cooperate with the Spirit. The same chapter in the Bible that talks about the fruit of the Spirit tells us to "walk by the Spirit" (verse 16, NIV 2011). Kindness is one of the easiest and best ways to walk by the Spirit and to let other people know we are Christians. A little act of kindness doesn't take a lot of effort, but it will mean so much to someone.

One time when my little sister, Bella, was younger, Two-Mama was really excited because she was going to get to go to Las Vegas with my mom, my dad, and Two-Papa, to a trade show for Duck Commander. But Bella got the flu the day before Two-Mama planned to fly out. My mom was already in Las Vegas because she had to be out there a day earlier to set up for the show. Well, Two-Mama could not bear to leave Bella with a babysitter when she had the flu, so she decided to stay home. John Luke and I were there too.

The way Two-Mama tells the story, John Luke disappeared for a little while one afternoon while she was keeping us. She knew he was in the house and safe, but he was very quiet. He later walked up to her and handed her a bouquet of flowers made of pipe cleaners. This homemade gift (showing his artistic side!) was his way of telling Two-Mama he knew she had made a sacrifice in order to stay home, and he loved and appreciated her for doing that. He didn't have the words to express what was in his heart, so he put his heart into a bouquet of flowers, and Two-Mama knew exactly what he was trying to tell her. That's one of her favorite examples of kindness.

Another one of her favorite stories is about a time when she ended up babysitting five toddlers for a whole weekend. (Two-Mama babysits a *lot*!) There was a moment when all five were crying and needing things at the same time, and Two-Mama was pretty stressed about it. In fact, she says that whole day was totally stressful for lots of reasons.

John Luke was with her, and he was older than the other children. She says he followed her around that day very patiently, not asking for anything. She felt bad because she could not give him much attention. Later, she even told him she was sorry she had not been able to do much with him that day, and maybe they could spend more time together the next day.

The next morning, Two-Mama got up and saw a message in soap-crayon on her bathroom mirror. It simply said: "I love you, 2-Mama."

John Luke had written it the night before. When Two-Mama tells this story, she always makes it a point to say that John Luke did not tell her about the message when he wrote it. He could see she was busy and stressed, so he just did it and then waited patiently for her to find it. For him, that act of kindness was not about being praised for doing something nice; it was about blessing his tired grandmother!

I was the one to receive kindness one night last year when I had had "one of those days." I had so much to do, and I was super stressed about it. I'm sure lots of teenagers can relate to that. I had to stay up really late that night trying to finish my homework, and I was so upset about the pressure that I ended up crying and feeling completely overwhelmed.

When I finally got ready to go to bed, which was probably sometime really early in the morning, I found a note from Bella on my pillow. The note had a Bible verse and a message about how much she loved me and hoped I was not stressed (which I was, totally). That made my night—and the whole next day. I basically forgot about the stress and could not think about anything but how sweet Bella was to write me that note.

Bella was pretty young when she left the note for me, only ten years old. But even at that age, she knew how to be kind. No one has to wait until they get older to be kind! Besides that, Bella did not have to spend a lot of time or money to write me that little note. It only took her a couple of minutes, and she did it with a piece of paper and a pen she found around our house. I say this to make the point that kindness can be quick, easy, and inexpensive. All it takes is a heart that cares about other people.

> Kindness can be quick, easy, and inexpensive. All it takes is a heart that cares about other people.

Another example of kindness comes from my brother Will. He and Bella ride with me to school every morning. Believe it or not, between John Luke and me, I am actually the better driver, so they like riding with me. Every morning during the wintertime, Will gets ready and goes outside in the cold to turn on the car and get it warmed up for me. I did not realize how awesome that really is until one morning after Will had spent the night with a friend and I had to get in the freezing-cold car and sit in the driveway waiting for the windshield to defrost before I could drive to school. When he came home, I made it a point to tell him how much I appreciated his doing that special act of kindness every morning to help my day start off warm and toasty.

# THINK ABOUT OTHERS

All my life, Two-Papa has had a great way of doing acts of random kindness. He gives away one-hundred-dollar bills to people in need. He does it anonymously (though some people will find out about it in this book), and he does it for only one reason: he genuinely wants to make people happy.

One time, he walked by an old car in a Walmart parking lot and just happened to look inside. Among all the trash on the front seat, he saw a bill from the electric company and realized the person's electricity was about to be cut off. The bill happened to be just under a hundred dollars. He put a hundred-dollar bill on the seat under the electric bill and went on his way.

Another time, he gave everyone in our church youth group one hundred dollars at Christmastime. But there was a catch: they could not keep the money; they had to give it to someone else. After Christmas, the group got together and everyone had to say what they did with the money. There were stories of teenagers who bought groceries for families, paid bills, and got toys for children who would not have had toys at Christmastime otherwise.

That Christmas, Two-Papa really gave the youth group a better gift than anything money could buy, definitely worth more than one hundred dollars. He taught them the importance of thinking about others and he gave them the resources to find out how good it feels to do something for someone else.

## KINDNESS MADE THE DIFFERENCE

Years ago, when my papaw Phil fished to support his family, he had to be very serious about his fishing, and he carefully guarded the river near his house.

Some local boys started making trouble one day when they stole some of his fish. Then they came back another day, and another day. It really got to be a problem. Papaw Phil finally went outside with a shotgun and yelled that he would shoot them if they did not get off his property—for good! Papaw Phil and his shotgun would have scared a lot of people away, but not those boys. They kept coming back.

During this time, Papaw Phil became a Christian, and the next time they came back, instead of going outside with his gun, he took his Bible. He walked over to them and said, "Whatever fish you have, you can keep. But you have to come to my house and have a Bible study with me."

They did, and they never stole from him again. The shotgun did not keep those boys away, but kindness got the job done.

## IT'S GOT TO BE GENUINE

I hope it's clear by now that acts of random kindness do not have to be big things—like my boyfriend's willingness to risk ruining his car. What they *do* have to be is genuine. If not, they feel a little bit cheesy and empty to people. Whatever you do to be kind to people will usually make a positive impression on them, but what really makes a big impact is the genuineness and sincerity in your heart when you do it. Look people in the eye when you do something nice for them and say, "God bless you"—and mean it. Whatever you do, it needs to come from a place inside of you that wants to honor God and bless other people.

Ever since I saw *Evan Almighty*, the whole idea of acts of random kindness has stuck with me. As I have tried to do nice, unexpected things for people, I have learned that it's important to always be ready to help, no matter where you are—and it's important to have a smile on your face when you do it. If you do something helpful, but you sigh and roll your eyes and act bothered about it, the action may not be genuinely kind. And people know it. They also know when you are sincere.

You might get some hate when you extend kindness to people. They may wonder what you want from them, or they may find some other reason to question whether you are sincere or not. Just shake that off and be kind anyway.

# DO IT NOW

I recently heard about a story on a Christian radio station. The host talked about a man somewhere in America who realized that people offered to help him pretty often. He was thinking about people in stores who say, "May I help you?" or maybe even people at places like the post office or a library. He also realized he almost always said no when people offered to help.

So he decided to start saying yes—not just sometimes, but every time someone asked, "May I help you?"

One day a man at the grocery store said, "Can I take your groceries to your car?"

He said yes.

He tried to tip the man, but the man refused to take any money and started telling a story.

The man had been diagnosed with cancer about fifteen years earlier, and the doctors only gave him a short time to live. For some reason, though, he was one of those people who outlived his diagnosis—by something like fifteen years at that point. When he got past the time the doctors said he would live, he decided to spend the rest of his life helping people, every way he could. That's how he ended up working at the grocery store. The job gave him a chance to help people every single day.

My youth minister at church says people sometimes wait until something bad happens to someone before they do nice things for that person. Maybe someone on your sports team has an injury and everyone seems to really care about that person when he or she is hurt, but no one has taken an interest before. I have decided that I want to make a difference while the good stuff is happening; I don't want to wait until someone is in a bad situation to start doing nice things. I hope you won't wait either. Let's get busy together and do some acts of random kindness—with genuineness and sincerity—right now.

# Live Original Challenge

1. Has someone ever done an act of random kindness for you? What was it, and how did it make you feel?

_____

_____

_____

_____

2. Is there someone at your school or in your family who would really appreciate an act of random kindness? Who is it, and what could you do for that person?

_____

_____

_____

3. What can you do anonymously to bless or encourage someone?

_____

_____

_____

4. List three ways you could make someone's day today.

_____

_____

_____

## DON'T FORGET

**Do acts of random kindness
every time you have a chance!**

*But to you who are willing to listen, I say, love your enemies!*
*Do good to those who hate you.*
*Bless those who curse you.*
*Pray for those who hurt you.*

—Luke 6:27–28

# CHAPTER EIGHT

## Shake the Hate

Our family gets a lot of invitations to do media appearances. Some people genuinely respect us and some are just *really* curious about us. The first time the men in the family were asked to be guests on one of the late-night talk shows, a musical group had also been invited to be part of the lineup. When they found out they would appear the same night as Papaw Phil and the rest of the guys, they refused to play. They did not seem to object to our Christian beliefs or our politics; they had an issue with hunting animals.

I guess animal rights activists would have a problem with Papaw Phil; I get that. In our family, we view hunting and fishing as part of the circle of life, part of God's design for us to eat and survive on this earth. If you have watched *Duck Dynasty* very much, you have probably seen how crazy Mamaw Kay is about her dogs, Jesse and Bobo; they are like part of the family. In fact, a lot of us Robertsons are animal lovers. We have lots of pets and we take great care of them. But the musical guests did not understand that.

When the host interviewed Papaw Phil and asked him how he felt about the fact that the band would not appear with him, he had a simple answer: "We just love 'em anyway."

Just loving people anyway is the best response to hate. And hate seems to be happening more and more, especially among high school students. But even elementary school children experience bullying in school. It's becoming a big problem. I guess one way to deal with hate is to give hate back, but a better way is to shake it off and love people anyway. 1 Peter 3:9 says,

> *Don't repay evil for evil.*
> *Don't retaliate with insults when people insult you.*
> *Instead, pay them back with a blessing.*
> *That is what God has called you to do,*
> *and he will grant you his blessing.*

# IT'S HAPPENED TO ME

When I was about fifteen or sixteen, some people in my own hometown were saying negative things about me. They were simply making stuff up; it wasn't even true! People make stuff up about people in the spotlight all the time.

Have you ever heard the saying "If you stick your neck out, be prepared for someone to try to chop it off"? That's true. It happens. Through reading made-up stuff about us, my family has learned not to believe everything we read or hear in magazines, online, or on television. We have found that if an article or report says, "sources reveal," or "sources close to the family say," those words are just code for "We totally made this up."

Well, that was happening in my own hometown. People at other schools, who had never met me and knew absolutely nothing about me, were saying things about me. During this time, some of the people close to me felt the need to tell me every hurtful thing others said about me, and it really started getting to me.

One day someone came up to me and said, "I need to tell you something So-and-So is saying about you."

I replied, "Is it going to hurt my feelings?"

She said, "Yes, but I really need to tell you."

I said, "No, you don't."

She went on to say she really thought I needed to know this, to which I continued to reply, "No, I don't."

I eventually just walked away.

My mom was surprised when I told her this. She said most teenagers and even adults would feel like they just *had* to know, but that I showed real maturity in just walking away. I didn't think it was maturity as much as self-preservation! I know myself, and if I allow myself to hear negativity from others, it will really hurt me. It will bother me, make me want to change who I am, and make me scared to "stick my neck out." I know God does not want that out of me, so I simply "shake the hate" and walk away when necessary.

> If an article says, "sources reveal," or "sources close to the family say," those words are just code for "We totally made this up."

If we listen to hate, what will happen? It will eventually go to our minds. We will start questioning things about ourselves. We will wonder, *Am I skinny enough? Smart enough? Athletic enough? Funny enough?* And the list goes on and on. We will become very negative and probably try to bring others down with us. And that's the last thing we should do.

Some haters are going to hate no matter what. That happens in person, and it happens on social media. Our family gets some hate from people on social media, and my mom and I have learned to just accept what people say and not get down about it. Sometimes, we just laugh, shake our heads, and move on. One time I told my mom someone on social media said I looked like a man in one of my pictures. She said, "Well, someone said I look like Squidward from *SpongeBob SquarePants.* Top that!" And we had a good laugh about it.

Maybe this happens to us more than it happens to some people because we are on television. But I know it happens to everyone, especially high school students. Unfortunately, there is just a lot of hate that goes around! I have seen a simple comment about a football game lead to people posting incredibly hateful things to someone. It's amazing what people can find to be hateful about.

For some people, even trying to do the things I have mentioned in this book so far may get a little hate. Not everyone will like it when you start thinking positively and being happy, or when you begin to develop confidence. The only advice I have about that is to just be yourself, don't let people intimidate you, and keep doing the right thing, even when it's hard.

## TALK TO YOURSELF

The easiest thing to do when people start hating on us or being unkind is to be hurt and to get angry with them. We are tempted to think about how mean they are and wonder what is wrong with them. We can quickly accuse them of negative things as we try to defend ourselves.

What we tell ourselves when other people start being hateful or disrespectful to us is very important. I have learned that the first thing I need to do is ask myself, "What would cause someone to say that?" I can't ask that question every time someone says anything negative, because I do get some hate on social media, and I don't pay attention to it because it comes from people I do not even know. I cannot obsess over people I have never met or even over very casual acquaintances, but all of us have to respect and value closer relationships enough to want to know what's going on with a person if they are not being nice. If the person bothering me is a close friend, someone at school, or someone I know, I do wonder about their reason for being negative toward me. I think, *Is that person having a bad day? Has something happened recently in their life, their family, or a relationship that would make them envious of me, my life, or my relationships?* I wonder if something is going on in their lives—something that has nothing to do with me—and maybe they are taking out their anger on me. Or maybe, I think, they could be insecure and trying to bring me down with them. Some people cut others down to try to feel better about themselves. This obviously does not work. It's one of Satan's traps, but unfortunately it is one many people fall into. The most important question I ask myself is this: *Am I doing something that would cause a person to say or do something hurtful to me?* I really try to be nice to everyone, but all of us can accidentally offend people or hurt their feelings. We all make mistakes and do not always say or do the right things. When that happens, we need to be aware of it and honest about it. We should admit it and apologize.

There's usually a reason people do what they do, especially when they are unkind. Sometimes, the reason is something only they know or only their family knows, but it's really bugging them and causing them to act in unusual ways. They might not even know they are doing it.

When someone hates on you, talk to yourself before you talk back to them. You might learn something about yourself or realize something about them if you ask yourself the right questions—and it might help you make the situation better instead of worse.

I really like the Bible verses that say,

> *Why worry about a speck in your friend's eye*
> *when you have a log in your own . . .*
> *First get rid of the log in your own eye;*
> *then you will see well enough*
> *to deal with the speck in your friend's eye.*
> —Matthew 7:3–5, NIV

I can just see a big log sticking out of my eye, someone with a speck in theirs, and me trying to see around my log to pick it out! Sometimes we are quick to point out the problems in others while totally ignoring our own. The Bible warns us not to do that and gives us that great illustration so we won't forget.

> When someone hates on you, talk to yourself before you talk back to them.

## SOMETIMES, WHAT'S WRONG IS WHAT'S NOT RIGHT

When you ask yourself what you might have done wrong in a situation with someone who is being rude to you, it's important to also ask yourself another question. If you can honestly tell yourself you are not doing anything wrong, ask: "Am I doing enough right?" Let me explain.

One time a girl at school seemed to be really angry with me, and I could not figure out why. I had never gossiped about her; I did not steal her boyfriend; I did not get a role she wanted in the school play or beat her for a spot on a sports team. I had not said anything rude to her, and to the best of my knowledge I had not done a single thing to upset or offend her. I was really confused about why she acted so negatively toward me. It seemed so totally random.

I finally realized the problem wasn't that I was doing anything wrong; the problem was that I was not doing anything right. As I thought about that girl, I saw that I could have been more of a friend to her. I could have gone out of my way to include her, but I didn't. Some people don't think this is something they need to work on, but when I looked at myself, I thought it was. And to tell the truth, I think we all need to look at ourselves and see what we can do right. Now I try to make it my first instinct to do something right.

# IT'S NOT FUNNY IF IT HURTS

I can hardly believe some of the things that are on television and the Internet because people try to be funny. A lot of things in the media are not funny at all. Some are just plain disrespectful and hurtful. People often use sarcasm to make others laugh, but they do it at someone else's expense. But hurting someone's feelings is not funny.

My mom has always told my siblings and me not to use humor

to cut someone else down. My parents have taught us not to be critical or to make jokes about things people cannot help. They have taught us to be respectful of others. That includes not only using our manners but also being careful with our sense of humor.

Now, I know you may be thinking we do this a lot on *Duck Dynasty*. We make jokes about Jep being the baby of the family or about my dad for putting on a few extra pounds or Si for—well, for being Si. But the Robertson family has been taught not to take ourselves too seriously, to laugh at ourselves, and to laugh along with others. But there is a line that can be crossed, and because we are family, for the most part we know where that line is and we do not cross it.

We would never want to make a joke about someone that would hurt that person's feelings. We need to be aware of others' feelings and cautious about how we joke and whom we joke with. There is a proverb that warns us about the destructiveness of "joking":

> *Like a maniac shooting flaming arrows of death*
> *is one who deceives their neighbor and says,*
> *"I was only joking!"*
> —Proverbs 26:18–19, NIV 2011

We must be careful to not throw flaming arrows.

My mom's grandmother, my mamaw Jo, is in her eighties, and she has lived a great life. People love her, and you will never hear an unkind word about her. For as long as my mom can remember, Mamaw Jo has said, "Nothing is worth hurting someone's feelings over."

Some people get their feelings hurt over the slightest thing, so we can't always do this perfectly, but I think Mamaw Jo has a good point. People are too important to be the butts of jokes or sarcasm.

Everybody is valuable, and we need to use words to encourage and affirm them, not to criticize them or hurt them.

# EVEN A PERFECT PERSON DIDN'T ESCAPE THE HATE

When you think about how long people have been living on earth and how many people have lived, it blows your mind. That's *a lot* of people! But only one of all the millions and millions who have ever lived was perfect. Jesus was perfect; He never sinned (see 1 Peter 2:22). Hebrews 4:15 talks about Jesus being our high priest and says, "This high priest of ours understands our weaknesses, for he faced all of the same testings we do, yet he did not sin." The fact that Jesus did not sin is what makes Him perfect. No one before Him and no once since then has ever been flawless, though I have met a few people who seem to think they are!

Even though Jesus was perfect, He still had haters—some who hated Him intensely. Luke 7:33–34 says Jesus and John the Baptist could not please everyone: "For John the Baptist didn't spend his time eating bread or drinking wine, and you say, 'He's possessed by a demon.' The Son of Man [Jesus], on the other hand, feasts and drinks, and you say, 'He's a glutton and a drunkard, and a friend of tax collectors and other sinners!'" In other words, no matter what Jesus or John the Baptist did, someone found a reason to criticize them.

The hate against Jesus eventually became so strong that people put Him to death—not just any kind of death; they killed Him by one of the cruelest methods possible. They put nails through His hands and feet and hung Him on a cross. He agreed to suffer this kind of death because it was God's plan. It was the way Jesus could pay for all our sins and give us eternal life. His death was full of hate from people but full of love from Him to us.

If the only perfect person to ever walk the earth got hate, you and I can be sure we will too. We could spend our time and energy trying to keep it from happening, but the truth is, it's going to happen. We would be much better off to spend our time figuring out how to deal with it in ways that please God when it does.

> Jesus' death was full of hate from people but full of love from Him to us.

## DON'T LET HATE HAPPEN

Learning to handle the hate that may come against you is a big job, and it takes some maturity. But I think we need to do even more than that. We not only need to make sure we shake the hate in our own lives, we also need to look out for other people and help them stand strong.

Whenever people get hate, it's important for someone to be there with them. That way, they feel supported and they do not feel alone. Sometimes we do this in person, like if something happens at school. Another way to stand up for people is to delete hurtful things we see on social media. If people can't see the hate, they can't keep it going.

As I said earlier, haters are going to hate. But good people do not have to put up with it. The only way hate will ever get better is for people to stand up against it and shake it off. You can do that, and I can do that. And together, we can make the world a nicer, kinder, friendlier place.

# Live Original Challenge

1. Is there someone in your life who gets a lot of hate? How can you stand up for that person?

_____

_____

_____

2. How can you start talking to yourself differently when people hate on you?

_____

_____

_____

3. Think about some of the people who may be causing you trouble. If you have not done anything wrong to them, what can you start doing right?

_____

_____

_____

4. If you have been sarcastic in the past, I challenge you to be funny without being hurtful. What can you do to take the challenge?

_____

_____

_____

## DON'T FORGET

**Hate will cause you to become negative if you let it, so don't. Shake it off!**

*A friend loves at all times.*

—Proverbs 17:17, NIV

# CHAPTER NINE

## A Friend's a Friend Forever

No matter how different church groups and Christian school groups are, they have one thing in common: they play a certain Michael W. Smith song for graduating seniors—and almost everybody cries. Maybe you know what I'm talking about. The song is called "Friends Are Friends Forever." Basically, it says that even close friends sometimes have to separate—maybe to go to college or to move away from one place to take a job somewhere else—and it says that when God is the Lord of our friendships, we can be friends for the rest of our lives.

If you are anything like me, your friendships are a huge part of your life. I want to be with my friends all the time, and I love having them over to our house. I have a great group of friends. One of the best parts of our group friendship is that we are in different grades at school. One girl graduated last year and is a freshman in college, three of us are sophomores, and three are seniors. One of the girls in this group is my very best friend and has been since prekindergarten. People at school call us "PBJ," because we are together so much, like peanut butter and jelly. All of us are very close—pretty much inseparable.

I like my friends so much because they are very spiritual girls. We make an effort to encourage each other, and to listen to, care about, and support each other. Sometimes, we just send texts to share a scripture or some other kind of positive, uplifting thought, and sometimes we stay up until three or four in the morning, just talking and encouraging each other. We rarely fight; we do our best not to get jealous of each other; we celebrate the happy things in each other's lives, and we are there for the sad things. This is the way I think friendship should be, and if a friend is a friend forever, these are the kinds of friends I want.

Unfortunately, friendship is not always this way, especially in high school. Too many people end up with too much drama. There's jealousy and gossip and all kinds of negativity—and those things will kill a friendship fast.

> You have the potential to be a great friend, and if you are a great friend, you'll have great friends in return.

Growing up is not always easy. I like having good directions, and the best directions I know are in the Bible. It gives us a lot of instructions to help us have good friendships and be good friends. Ephesians 4:31–32 covers all the basics: "Get rid of all bitterness, rage, anger, harsh words, and slander, as well as all types of evil behavior. Instead, be kind to each other, tenderhearted, forgiving one another, just as God through Christ has forgiven you."

In this chapter, I hope to share some stories and truths that will help you make your friendships better—whether they are pretty good already or whether you feel like you need a lot of help. I believe you have the potential to be a great friend, and if you are a great friend, you'll have great friends in return.

# HOW TO BE A GOOD FRIEND

Relationships are about choices. Just think about it: we choose who we want to be friends with, we choose how we act toward other people, and we choose how we respond when others do unkind things to us. You can make all kinds of choices in friendship; some will make your friendships better and some will make your friendships worse. In the next section, I'll mention some things not to do if you want to be a good friend. But first I want to write about some positive choices you can make in your efforts to have good, strong, long-lasting friendships. These guidelines work just as well in boyfriend-girlfriend relationships as they do in other friendships.

Choose not to argue over stupid stuff. When teenagers or middle schoolers get together, sometimes stupid things happen. People do not always think about the consequences of their words or actions, and pretty soon an argument is going full blast.

My friends and I have seen this happen many times, and we made an important decision about it. When we have different opinions on a situation, before we let an argument start, we ask, "Is it worth it, or do we just want to argue?" It's not that speaking your mind is always bad. Everybody has intense feelings at times; the key is knowing what to do with them. Maybe we need to take them out on the basketball court, on a canvas, on a guitar, or in some other way that gets the feelings out without hurting other people.

Here's two of my favorite verses about this:

> Don't pick a fight without reason,
> when no one has done you harm.
> —Proverbs 3:30

111

*Don't get involved in foolish, ignorant arguments*
*that only start fights.*
*A servant of the Lord must not quarrel*
*but must be kind to everyone, be able to teach,*
*and be patient with difficult people.*
—2 Timothy 2:23–24

Both of these verses make the same point: don't argue over stupid stuff!

Choose to rejoice when your friend rejoices and to be sad when your friend is sad. One year I decided to try out for cheerleading at school. My best friend tried out too. She made the squad and was really excited about it. I did not make it, but I was still happy for her. I didn't want the fact that I didn't make it to be a concern for her. She earned it, and she deserved to celebrate. I wanted to celebrate with her.

That was the same year all of the *Duck Dynasty* stuff got crazy and busy, so God was watching over me and already had that planned. The next year my friend tried out again and I told her, "If you make it, we're going to do something really fun. If you don't make it, we're going to do something really fun." I know sometimes things like trying out for any kind of sport and not making it seem like the end of the world. But when God closes one door, He opens a better one.

Romans 12:15 says:

*Be happy with those who are happy,*
*and weep with those who weep.*

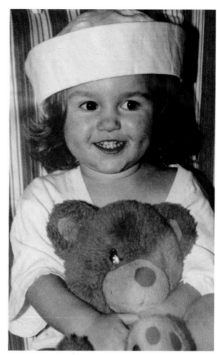

LEFT: My first official photo shoot at 3 months old. I was obviously happy about it. (1997)

ABOVE: My favorite teddy bear—I lost it and I still think Mom lost it on purpose because I was so attached to it. She swears she didn't. I was two years old. (1999)

ABOVE: Hanging out in my pj's with my dad and brother John Luke, on the back steps of our house. I was a year old. (1998)

RIGHT: John Luke and I both got a dollar from the bride for being in this wedding and for standing in my spot without crying. I did my job. (2000)

ABOVE: This is one of my favorite pictures of me and Mom. Enjoying time together on the porch after church on Sunday. (2001)

ABOVE: We spend a week at the beach every summer with our whole family. I love these trips and I love my Daddy. I was three years old. (2000)

LEFT: John Luke and I are twenty months apart and we have always been best friends. Well, most of the time. (Summer 2002)

LEFT: I loved to dress up. I was a very fashionable "mama." Bella was like a real-life baby doll. (2003)

RIGHT: I got Dad to dress up with me! I was Beauty, he was the Beast. (Halloween 2003)

LEFT: I love my Two-Mama. She's always there for her grandkids. The most selfless person I know. (Beach 2006)

ABOVE: My cousin Katelyn. She's a great friend and example to me. I always love being with her. (Camp Ch-Yo-Ca 2004)

RIGHT: I've always been into sports. Duck Commander was the sponsor for my softball team. (2007)

ABOVE: Two-Mama and I as the Good Witch and Dorothy. (Halloween 2003)

LEFT: My amazing great-grandmother, Mamaw Jo, with her favorite grandkids, me and Katelyn. (2014)

ABOVE: My roommate from Austria. Happy to say, we still keep in touch. That trip taught me a lot. (2009)

LEFT: Fifth grade. Fun photo shoot. (2008)

RIGHT: My sweet friend Yiekka and her little cousin in the Dominican Republic. (2011)

ABOVE: Every year around my birthday, I make a trip to Papasita's restaurant. Wearing a sombrero proudly. (2011)

LEFT: Papaw Phil and I filming for *Duck Dynasty*. The show has actually brought us even closer. (2012)

**ABOVE:** Surfing in Malibu. I look really confident in this picture but was actually scared to death. I don't like sharks. (2012)

**LEFT:** Reed and I after our team won state in track. I threw javelin. I got my throwing arm from my Papaw Phil. (2012)

**RIGHT:** Honored to be on the homecoming court at my school. I wore a dress from my Sherri Hill "Live Original" collection. My Two-Mama and Two-Papa are always there to support me. (2013)

**LEFT:** Me and my sweet mama. She's always by my side; my mom and my best friend. Plus, we share each other's clothes. (2013)

**RIGHT:** My dad escorted me across the football field homecoming night. I think he was wearing those glasses so nobody could see the tears. (2013)

ABOVE: So thankful to have this awesome group of friends. We will be friends forever. Steamboat Springs, Colorado. (2013)

ABOVE: Basketball is my sport. It's in my blood. My great-uncle is my coach and my whole family comes to cheer me on. One summer I shot a hundred free throws every day in my driveway. I thought: I'm never going to miss a free throw again.

RIGHT: The Duck Commander 500 at the Texas Motor Speedway. Pretty Cool! (2013)

ABOVE: Still can't believe I got to walk for New York Fashion Week! This was at the party Mrs. Sherri threw for me after the show. Plaza Hotel (2013) (Photograph by Henry S. Dziekan III/Getty Images)

RIGHT: The Robertson women take CMA Fest in Nashville! (2013)

LEFT: This little girl Maria, has had my heart since the first time I traveled to the Dominican when she was just five years old. (D.R. Trip. 2013)

RIGHT: Saying good-bye is always hard . . . until next year. (D.R. Trip 2013)

ABOVE: An ad for my line of Sherri Hill prom dresses. I really never dreamed this would happen! (2013) (Photograph © Dusty Hill, Sherri Hill, Inc.)

ABOVE: My Sweet Sixteen party. Junk Gypsy's decorated and Scotty McCreery sang. Friends and family were there. A night I'll never forget. (2013)

LEFT: Love my sisters! Rebecca, Bella, and me. (2014)

RIGHT: A fun photo shoot for my sister, Rebecca, and Mom's store, Duck & Dressing. (2014)

RIGHT: At the Nickelodeon Kid's Choice Awards. We had a blast. (2014)

ABOVE: I love playing on the tennis team with these two—Reed and John Luke. (2014)

ABOVE: My favorite people. Easter with the family. (2014)

It's clear: we're supposed to be happy and excited when our friends are happy and excited, and we're supposed to be sad with them when they are sad. Sharing people's feelings and being sensitive to them in these ways definitely strengthens friendships.

Choose activities that are good and fun for your friend and for you. If you are going to be friends with a person or a group, you will do a lot of things together. You can choose to do things that will be fun and good for you, or you can choose to do things that will get you in trouble. You get to decide. Nobody likes to be bored or to have a bad time, so when you are with your friends, choose to do things that are safe and respectful but also fun for everyone.

My friends and I enjoy being together because we do things that are just fun. We know what makes each other laugh without cutting anyone down or being sarcastic. We talk about things that are happy, we dance, we go out to eat at fun restaurants, we hang out and watch good movies, or we just sit around and talk. Of course, we are not perfect and we have all messed up, but we work toward bringing out the best in each other. Ephesians 5:4 says,

> There must not be any unclean speech
> or foolish talk or dirty jokes.
> All of them are out of place.
> Instead, you should give thanks.[7]

Sometimes, people think being a Christian means you don't get to do anything fun, but that is not true. It just means you choose your fun. Psalm 118:24 says, "This is the day the Lord has made. We will rejoice and be glad in it." That tells me I can be happy every single day. Proverbs 15:13 says, "A glad heart makes a happy face." So get your friends together and have a good time—and you can all put on your happy faces!

Choose to truly listen to what your friend says. Saying what we want to say and feeling that others are really listening to us is important to all of us. Most of us do not have any trouble being good talkers, but we may struggle a little to be good listeners, and that is just as important.

Our friends will go through hard times—and so will we. One of the best things we can do for our friends is listen to them, then let them know we have heard what they said and we care about how they feel. We don't need to rush them so we can say something; instead, we need to listen and pay attention before we respond. Most of the time, having someone who will really listen means more to a friend than someone who just wants to comment on the situation.

James 1:19 is a really good piece of advice:

> *Understand this . . .*
> *You must all be quick to listen,*
> *slow to speak, and slow to get angry.*

Do you see what this verse says? It says we need to listen quickly and speak slowly. That tells me we need to listen first and speak last.

Especially if we are in some kind of disagreement or misunderstanding, we need to listen before we talk. Proverbs 18:13 says,

> *Spouting off before listening to the facts*
> *is both shameful and foolish.*

Who wants to be ashamed and foolish? Not me!

Choose your friends wisely. Your friends are the people you hang out with, and if you are a teenager, you may spend more time with your friends than with any other group of people in your life. The people you hang around are the ones who influence you. If you have happy people in your life, you will be happy too. But if you let yourself be around people who are down on themselves, you will get down on yourself too. So you can see why choosing friends wisely is so important. Proverbs 13:20 says,

> *Walk with the wise and become wise;*
> *associate with fools and get in trouble.*

I don't want to get in trouble, so I am going to make the best choices I can make when I choose my close friends.

First Corinthians 15:33 says, "Bad company corrupts good character." In other words, even if you are a good person, you can lose your positive values and good character if you surround yourself with bad company. The opposite is also true. If you spend time with good people, they will build up your good character, helping you become an even stronger, better person.

In addition to the things above, there are other ways you can help yourself have great friendships: You can be nice to people; you can be helpful; you can pay sincere, noncheesy compliments. You can also encourage people, and you can be excited with them when they do something like make the honor roll, land a part in the school play, get on the homecoming court, finally have a starting position, or get admitted to the college where they really want to go.

When you choose friends, one of the best things to do is look for happy, positive people who will help you grow in your faith and who encourage you in your relationship with God. The most important friends you can have are the ones who encourage you spiritually and help you mature as a Christian. If that's what you build a friendship on, you have made a good choice.

# WHAT *NOT* TO DO IF YOU WANT GREAT FRIENDSHIPS

Besides all the things we can do to be a good friend, there are also a lot of things we can do to hurt the friendships we already have or to keep ourselves from finding new friends. I want to focus on three of them specifically. My mom calls these things "sins that can corrupt friendship." To "corrupt" just means to ruin, and these things will ruin friendships fast. The first one is jealousy, the second is pride, and the third is selfishness. I'm sure you know these words, but let me write a little bit about why they do so much damage to friendships.

Jealousy. Jealousy can tear people apart like nothing else. It's very dangerous in a friendship. Here's some really strong statements from the Bible:

> *A peaceful heart leads to a healthy body;*
> *jealousy is like cancer in the bones.*
> —Proverbs 14:30

> *For wherever there is jealousy and selfish ambition,*
> *there you will find disorder and evil of every kind.*
> —James 3:16

I warned you that those verses were strong! We need to take them seriously and make a real effort to avoid being jealous of anyone, over anything.

When we are friends with someone, we should be happy for each other, no matter what happens. If someone gets a better grade than you, be happy. If someone gets the car you have been wanting for years, be happy. If someone gets a college scholarship you were hoping for, congratulate them—and mean it. When good things happen to your friends, be right there with them and celebrate with them the way you would want them to celebrate with you. Sometimes good things will happen to you; sometimes they won't. When they don't, be mature enough to refuse to be jealous or angry.

When I didn't make cheerleading, I could have been jealous; thinking only about my own feelings and getting stuck in disappointment would have been easy. But instead, I chose to be happy for my best friend and to celebrate with her. We both got to be happy over the good news when she made it. I said to her, "When there's a ball game, you cheer with the uniform and I will cheer in the stands, and we will have an awesome year." That's exactly what's happening.

I want to say one thing about friends and boyfriends. Your friends are your friends. They are not people you may date for a while and then break up with. Your real friends will always be there for you. Especially if you are a teenage or preteenage girl reading this, remember that boyfriends come and go, but a friend can be a friend forever. Jealousy, especially jealousy over guys, really just gets in the way. A friend may date someone you dated previously. It happens. Make a decision right now to keep your friendships in good shape and not let jealousy ruin them.

Pride. Nobody wants to hang out with people who think they are better than others. That's a major turnoff. I learned a long time ago that the best way to live is to put God first, other people second, and ourselves last. This is a great set of priorities—and if these three things are in order, the way we treat people and the way we act in general should prove that God really is first and that we really do care more about other people than about ourselves. Instead of always trying to get our way, we let others have their way. Instead of having to be right, we accept that others also have good points to make and opinions that matter.

Romans 12:3 says:

*Don't think you are better than you really are.*

This does not mean you get down on yourself and lose your confidence (because remember, confidence is key). There's nothing wrong with doing something well and feeling good about it. But feeling good about something and being proud about it are two different things. People who are proud think they are better than others. They have a big head about who they are and what they can do—but sometimes they are not all that great and other people are not all that bad. Everyone is valuable; everyone can do something well; everyone is important to God.

James 4:6 says,

*"God opposes the proud*
*but gives grace to the humble."*

If God opposes the proud, then proud is something I do not want to be! I want God's grace in my life, and the way to get it is by being humble—the exact opposite of being proud.

Selfishness. Most of us have seen people who are selfish and self-centered. They want their own way, they don't want to share anything, and sometimes they think everyone else's job is to make them happy. That kind of attitude will destroy a friendship.

When selfishness is part of a relationship, one person usually ends up doing whatever he or she wants without considering what the other person wants to do. Selfish people insist that a whole group go along with them, even if others would rather do something else. They want to go to the restaurants they like, listen to the music they like, and hang out the way they like to hang out. They do not share the good things they have, and the fact that they could bless someone else never really occurs to them. They often give the impression that they think they are better than everyone else, so they should get to do whatever they want.

Philippians 2:3–4 basically communicates everything I believe about friendship:

> *Don't be selfish; don't try to impress others.*
> *Be humble, thinking of others as better than yourselves.*
> *Don't look out only for your own interests,*
> *but take an interest in others, too.*

If we can live by this verse, we can avoid bad friendships and enjoy great ones.

Sometimes, friends do get jealous and act prideful or selfish—often because they feel hurt or disappointed. When a friend acts this way, it hurts us too. We feel let down. As friends, the best thing we can do is understand and offer grace and forgiveness, just as we hope they will offer those things to us when we act out. No one is perfect; we all have moments of jealousy, pride, or selfishness, but we need to recognize those characteristics in ourselves and change them rather than living in those sins, which will be a curse to our friendships.

## OLD FRIENDS, NEW FRIENDS

I started this chapter talking about the fact that a friend is a friend forever. That's true. Some friends will stick with us for the rest of our lives, but that does not mean we should not make new friends. Two-Mama tells me not to ever close my heart, to always keep my heart and mind open to new people God will bring into my life.

> Two-Mama tells me to always keep my heart and mind open to new people God will bring into my life.

I go to a small Christian school—not a large high school with tons of people. At my school, making friends is pretty easy. Of course, everyone is not best friends with everyone else, but we all know each other's names and we're friendly. I also have friends from camp. I have known many of those people since I was very young, so I consider them old friends.

Last year some new girls, two sisters, came to my school and I got to know them. They are two of my best friends now. They have become part of my group of close friends. If my old friends and I had not been willing to open our hearts to new friends, we would have missed knowing two amazing people who have brought good things into our lives.

Friendships are gifts from God. It's up to us to take them seriously and treat our friends well. We need to value our old friends, make room for new ones, and commit to being a great friend to all.

# *Live Original Challenge*

1. Who are your best friends?

_____

_____

_____

2. Think of three of the best friends you have and write down their best qualities or three reasons you are friends with them.

_____

_____

_____

3. In your own words, why are jealousy, pride, and selfishness dangerous to a
friendship?

_____

_____

_____

_____

4. What are one or two things about yourself that you can work on if you want
to be a better friend?

_____

_____

_____

## DON'T FORGET

**You can be a great friend!**

*Do to others whatever you would like them to do to you.*

—Matthew 7:12

# CHAPTER TEN

# *Respect Relationships*

Relationships. Everybody has them. Sometimes they are great, and sometimes they are not so great. They can be our biggest blessings or they can cause our biggest problems. There are thousands of books available on how to make relationships better. That tells me a *lot* of people think they need a *lot* of help knowing how to deal with others.

In *The People Factor*, Pastor Van Moody writes:

> You have some kind of relationship with everyone you encounter. . . . Some are casual and on-the-surface relationships, and some are intimate and deep. But every relationship you have influences your life. There are no neutral relationships. Each one lifts you up or weighs you down. It moves you forward or holds you back. It helps you or it hurts you.[8]

I've written some things in this book that make the same point Mr. Moody makes; I just worded them differently. Basically, he and

I are both saying that who we hang around with is important. The people we spend our time with have a major impact on us; they can make us better, more positive, more godly people, or they can make us worse, more negative people and pull us away from our relationship with God. Mr. Moody says, "Any relationship that pulls us away from God, His Word or His plan for our lives has to be put aside."[9] Yep. I totally agree with that.

God gives us people and relationships to help us. Sometimes we make bad choices and end up with the wrong people, but if we follow God in our relationships, we will end up with the right people. We need to appreciate and invest in those relationships. We also need to respect them, and that's what I want to write about now.

In this chapter I want to focus on four types of relationships we should respect:

1. Our relationships with our brothers and sisters

2. Our relationships with friends, boyfriends, and teammates

3. Our relationships with parents and authority figures

4. Our relationship with ourselves

## YOUR CLOSEST RELATIVES

Do you know the closest relatives you can ever have are your biological brothers and sisters? It's true. No matter how different you and they may seem, the fact is that you and your siblings have more DNA in common than you have with anyone else. All of you have DNA from both your parents—and that makes you more similar to your siblings than to anyone else in the whole world. This is why, when people need organ transplants, doctors first look for siblings as donors. They know a sibling is likely to be the best possible match.

Even if our DNA does not match, in the case of adopted siblings or stepbrothers and stepsisters, our siblings are usually the people we spend the most time with. We may share a room or a bathroom with them; we ride to and from school with them; we share meals and other family times with them. We are with our siblings a *lot*.

Since our brothers and sisters are usually the people we spend the most time with, we might think siblings would have close, strong, fun, peaceful relationships. That's not always true. I am shocked and sad when I hear stories about how harsh siblings are to each other. Of course, siblings are going to argue and pick on each other every now and then, but I can't imagine where I would be without my siblings. They teach me new things every day. I think teenagers need to understand how much of a blessing their siblings are, and we need to fight less and love more.

Sometimes, relationships end up bad because people don't know they can be good. I think as teenagers we have bought into the lie that we are *supposed* to fight with our siblings. There have been examples of siblings fighting since the beginning of time—Cain and Abel, Jacob and Esau, Rachel and Leah, and the list goes on.

But I'm telling you, it doesn't have to be that way. God calls us to love our brothers and sisters:

> *This is the message you heard from the beginning:*
> *We should love one another.*
> *Do not be like Cain, who belonged to the evil one*
> *and murdered his brother.*
> —1 John 3:11–12, NIV

*Whoever claims to know God yet hates*
*a brother or sister is a liar.*
*For whoever does not love their brother and sister,*
*whom they have seen,*
*cannot love God, whom they have not seen.*
*And he has given us this command:*
*Anyone who loves God must also love their brother and sister.*
—1 John 4:20–21, NIV 2011

Wow, those are pretty powerful words. It doesn't get any clearer than that. God expects us to *love* our siblings. But what if we do not feel like loving them? What if our brother or sister is not very lovable at the moment? Maybe he or she is straight-up acting like a brat? Well, God's Word has that covered too. It tells us what it really means to love. It tells us how to act in loving ways even when we do not feel love or even when the other person doesn't deserve it. The Bible tells us:

*Love is patient, love is kind.*
*It does not envy, it does not boast, it is not proud.*
*It does not dishonor others, it is not self-seeking,*
*it is not easily angered, it keeps no record of wrongs.*
*Love does not delight in evil but rejoices with the truth.*
*It always protects, always trusts,*
*always hopes, always perseveres.*
—1 Corinthians 13:4–7, NIV

Can you imagine how much better our relationships would be if we actually put this type of love into practice? If you want to have great relationships, this is how you do it. I challenge you to start loving your siblings today like the Bible defines love in 1 Corinthians 13. It will change everything.

Maybe you have not ever seen a strong example of a good sibling relationship. That's why I want to write about the great relationship I have with my brother John Luke. I hope these insights into our relationship will show you that siblings can get along, help each other, support each other, and be really important in each other's lives. Having great relationships with siblings, and everyone in our family, is so important. They are the people who will be there for us when no one else is.

Like a lot of children, probably *most* children, John Luke and I fought when we were little. But now we are best friends. Seriously. I know that may be hard for some people to believe, but it's true. My relationship with him is a big reason I am who I am today. He is one of the strongest Christian guys I know, and we lean on each other a lot.

John Luke and I are the type of best friends who hang out together at night and talk about everything that went on during the day. We have a lot of fun together. If one of us is bored, we call the other one and go play tennis or go to a movie or grab something to eat.

> When John Luke wants to ask a girl out, he says I have to approve of her. He knows I pick good ones!

I give him girl advice; he gives me boy advice—and I know he will be genuine and tell me the truth. He is also very protective of me where guys are concerned, and I really appreciate that. He knows what's good for me.

When John Luke wants to ask a girl out, he says I have to approve of her. He knows I pick good ones! But more than that, he knows I really care about him and want the best for him. I do not want him to get involved with someone who is not good for him, and he feels the same way about me.

John Luke and I are very close in age. He's only a year and a half older than I am and just one grade ahead of me in school. As I said, when we were young, we argued a lot, but our mom did *not* put up with that. She was definitely the parent! When we fought, she made us go sit in the same room together. She did not care who did what; we were *going* to get along. Whatever had happened, we had to work it out. I'm sure my mom knew that making us deal with each other and figure out our conflicts together would help us get along well and be friends later on. And that's exactly what happened.

I mentioned that I grew up doing a lot of things with John Luke and our cousins Reed and Cole. People in the family referred to us as "Sadie and the boys," so I learned about family relationships pretty early in my life. The boys and I had to learn to get along when we worked for Duck Commander and when we hung out at Papaw Phil and Mamaw Kay's house (she would not put up with fussing or fighting either; she sent us outside).

We also played a lot of football. In fact, I ended up with such a good arm that our school football coaches wanted me to play quarterback for the team when I was in seventh grade. My mom said no to that idea. The point is that I have always had opportunities to be around John Luke and get to know him in all kinds of settings. He's not as good an athlete as I am, but he never lets that bother him. He has always cheered me on, and I have always supported and encouraged him in the things he does well.

When people started hating on me (I wrote about that in chapter 8), John Luke was the one who stopped it. He stood up for me, and that gave me the confidence I needed to then stand up for myself. Unfortunately, people do turn against us sometimes, especially in high school, but if you have a good relationship with a sibling, you can know that at least one person is rooting for you. Sometimes that one person makes all the difference. I know John Luke is there for me, no matter what, and that makes my life a whole lot easier.

Even though I have written a lot about John Luke in this chapter, that does not mean I don't have great relationships with my other siblings. There is something special about my relationship with each one of them. I am the middle child, so I pull us all together. In this chapter I chose to write about John Luke because we are the closest in age, and sometimes the sibling who's closest in age is the one people tend to fight with most. I want people to know it does not have to be that way.

## MEAN WHAT YOU SAY

In relationships, one of the best qualities a person can have is integrity. This is true in relationships with all kinds of people—with friends or teachers and coaches at school or church, with coworkers, and with your family. If you have integrity, people know they can trust you, and that's really important. Being a person of integrity means being honest about everything, even when telling the truth does not make you look good. It also means you have the character to do the right thing, even when doing the right thing is hard or costs you something. When you have integrity, you take your commitments seriously. If you say you will be somewhere at a certain time, you show up. If you tell people you will do them a favor, you do it. People of integrity do not look for excuses, they find ways to keep their word, and that helps make their relationships strong. A pastor named David Jeremiah has a great quote: "Integrity is keeping a commitment even after circumstances have changed." That's not easy to do. I had to put this principle into practice a couple of weeks before I started writing this book.

On Valentine's Day weekend, I had a plane ticket to go see my boyfriend, who lives in another state, and I was so excited. I play on my school basketball team, but we did not have a game scheduled that weekend. There was no reason I could not make the trip. But then something came up. One of our weekday games got moved to Saturday!

I could not believe it. I was so upset! Now, don't get me wrong, basketball is my sport. I love it, but I did not want to give up my Valentine's Day plans to play in a game I knew would not be challenging or exciting. The team we had to play had only won two games all season, and I was confident our team could beat them without me.

But being on a team means being committed to other players. The whole point of being part of a group is that everybody gives everything they can give to help each other succeed. You cannot be on a team and then decide to participate only when it's convenient or when you don't have anything better to do.

> You cannot be on a team and then decide to participate only when it's convenient or when you don't have anything better to do.

I definitely thought going to see my boyfriend was better than playing basketball when my team did not need me. But because of the relationships I have with my teammates and my commitment to the team, I decided to ask them whether or not they were willing to play the game without me. Five girls on the team basically said, "We got this. Go see your boyfriend and have a great time."

One girl said, "You need to stay."

I did not want to hear *that*!

But I had made a commitment to the team and that girl was part of the team. Since the group decision was not unanimous, I knew I had to stay home and play the game. Changing my plans cost me money (to change my ticket) and was inconvenient. It also made me sad and angry, but I respected my team and I honored the commitment I had made to them.

My mom knew I was not happy, and she told me there was no point in having a bad attitude about the situation. Once I made my decision, she said, I needed to get over it. So I made lemonade. You know the old saying "When life gives you lemons, make lemonade." So that's what I did, literally. I stood in our kitchen and squeezed lemons *fiercely*. The lemonade was pretty good, but mostly it gave me a chance to calm down and get some of my energy out. Then I was happy again.

I did get to go see my boyfriend a few days later, but since Valentine's Day was on Friday, I totally missed that. We still had fun once I got there—and after my team won the ball game. Better than all of that, though, I knew I had been a person of character and commitment, treating my teammates and myself with integrity.

Proverbs 20:11 says:

> *Even children are known by the way they act,*
> *whether their conduct is pure, and whether it is right.*

We need to act right, even when we would rather do something else and even when it's hard. We do not honor God by acting in ways that are wrong, but if we do the right thing, we ultimately feel good about ourselves, and most important, we please Him.

# WHO'S THE BOSS?

"Who's the boss?" is a question with a simple answer. God's the boss—of everything. Another way to say this is that God is the ultimate authority in the world and in our individual lives. The Bible talks a lot about "fearing God," but this does not mean to be afraid of Him; it means to respect His authority and have honor and reverence for Him. This is the only way to live a happy, blessed life.

The way we learn to respect God's authority is to respect the authority we see on earth—our parents and grandparents, aunts and uncles, teachers, coaches, church leaders, neighbors, basically anyone older than we are.

My mom says respect sometimes comes from the knowledge that people in authority want the best for you. If I did not respect my parents, I probably would not do what they tell me to do. The same is true with God. If I don't respect Him, I will not obey Him. And then I'll be in real trouble! According to the Bible, respecting God and respecting our parents are the two most important areas of respect for us as teenagers. Ephesians 6:1–3, NIV says,

> *Children, obey your parents in the Lord, for this is right.*
> *"Honor your father and mother"—*
> *which is the first commandment with a promise—*
> *"that it may go well with you and that*
> *you may enjoy long life on the earth."* [10]

If God thought enough of this whole idea of respecting parents to make it one of the Ten Commandments (see Exodus 20:12), it must be important!

We have to understand that God knows everything. He knows way more than we do, and when He tells us to do something, it's always for our good. We might not understand it at the time—and we might not like it—but if we believe God loves us and wants to bless us, we will do it. When it comes to our relationships with God and with our parents, we honor them by doing what they say even if we do not see things the way they do. We respect them enough to do what they say because we know they love us and are looking out for our best interests.

We need to respect our teachers too. This is a big thing for high school students. Sometimes teachers let us know they expect to be respected and sometimes they don't. But because they are teachers and we are students, we need to respect them anyway. We respect their positions of authority, even if we do not like the way they handle our classrooms.

One time I had a class that was always a little out of control. People who behaved well in other classes did not act nicely in this class. A few people showed respect to the teacher because of her position, but some walked all over her. She threatened different kinds of discipline but never followed through. This went on for a while, until the teacher finally got frustrated and asked us why we were so bad in her class.

No one said anything for a moment, then I spoke up. "Honestly, I don't think you expect us to respect you," I told her. "You say you aren't going to put up with things, and then you let us get away with them. You don't seem to expect respect, so we don't think we need to give it."

I'm not saying it was right for the students to treat her that way, but a fact of life is that if you don't expect other people to treat you with respect, in all likelihood, they won't. If you are a high school student, you can probably relate to this. Good students like teachers who make us respect them. If they do not act like they deserve or expect respect, most of the time they will not get it.

Even if you are young now, someday you will be older and have a position of authority. When you do, you will want people to respect you. You can prepare for that now by learning what respect means and showing it to everyone in authority over you.

# THE ONE PERSON YOU CAN NEVER GET AWAY FROM

There's one person in the world you can never escape, no matter how fast you run, where you try to hide, or how hard you work at it. You can never get away from yourself. That's why learning to respect yourself is one of the best things you can do. I'm not talking about having good self-esteem—"self-esteem" implies thinking highly of yourself. I'm talking about self-respect. Self-respect is knowing that Christ lives in you and that you belong to Him.

This is especially important in girlfriend/boyfriend relationships. If you do not let your boyfriend know from the very beginning that you expect to be treated with respect, just like the example of the teacher at my school, chances are, he won't treat you respectfully.

One time a guy asked me to be his girlfriend and I said, "Under one condition."

"What's that?" he asked.

I answered, "I ain't no hoochie mama, and you ain't about to make me one."

Okay, I know I'm not supposed to say "ain't," but I was making a point. I was sending him a strong message: "I have certain values and priorities, and you are not going to change me."

That was the only way a relationship with him would work. I would not let it be any other way. If he wanted a girl he did not have to respect, he needed to find someone else.

I really want to encourage girls my age to make it known right off the bat that they respect themselves. Telling a guy at the very beginning of a relationship that you respect yourself and that you expect him to respect you is way better than trying to say it later. When you are dealing with guys, get it out there early and get on the same page—and make it the page that says "Respect." That kind of respect for each other is what brings the best relationship.

> Telling a guy at the very beginning of a relationship that you respect yourself and that you expect him to respect you is way better than trying to say it later.

The same thing is true in friendships and other relationships. If you do not respect yourself, then no one else is going to respect you. Respect has to start with you. When people see that you will not put up with hate, bad language, negative talk, or people trying to take advantage of you, they will not treat you that way.

You are valuable! You are worth respecting. No matter what you may struggle with, you are still a person God made. You are His child. He loves you, and He has good plans for your life. If you respect yourself and insist that others respect you too, you'll be right in the middle of God's plans for your life now and on track for a great future.

# R-E-S-P-E-C-T

A long time ago, in 1967, Aretha Franklin put out a song that spells the word "respect," and it ended up being really popular. That song still plays today, and it's a good thing, because we all need to be reminded to be respectful, especially in relationships.

I hope your relationships will get better and better, whether you are dealing with siblings and family members; people to whom you have made commitments; authority figures, including God; parents; or yourself. If you respect others, they will respect you!

# Live Original Challenge

1. Do you stand up for your brothers and sisters? Next time someone starts hating on one of your siblings, what can you do to support them and protect them?

_____

_____

_____

2. Are you a person who keeps your commitments? How do you need to improve?

_____

_____

_____

3. Do you respect authority? In your own words, why is it important to do so?

_____

_____

_____

4. What is one thing you can do today to have a better relationship with yourself?

_____

_____

_____

_____

## DON'T FORGET

**Always respect your relationships.**

*Don't let anyone think less of you because you are young.*
*Be an example to all believers in what you say,*
*in the way you live, in your love,*
*your faith, and your purity.*

—1 Timothy 4:12

# CHAPTER ELEVEN

## Five Seconds of Awkward

I have lots of cousins. You see some of them on *Duck Dynasty*, but we have a really big family, with even more cousins you have not met on the show. I am especially close to my cousin Katelyn, who's on my mom's side of the family. My mom babysat her when she was young, and she was one of my babysitters when I was little. Now she is a mom herself and is a great example to me of what it means to be a woman of God. She gives great advice and said something at a Bible study one night that I don't think I will ever forget, something every teenager needs to hear: "Five seconds of awkward can save you from a lifetime of regret."

I know. That's powerful, right?

We have all had times when we feel awkward or insecure. Those experiences may or may not affect your everyday life. But here I'm talking about the times when something is happening that you know is not right, and you have to either walk away or speak up and stand up for what you believe. I'm talking about those moments you *know* will be awkward. People will notice when you suddenly leave a party or when you stop the gossip and say to your friends, "I don't think this is right." Or when your boyfriend tries to go too far and you have speak up and tell him to stop. Some of these situations could carry more weight than others in the long run of your life.

In those moments, we can make bad decisions or good ones. If we make the wrong choice, the rest of our life could be really hard. If we make the right choice, we will grow in confidence, strength, and maturity because we have taken a stand for godliness and strong character. And when we look back on these times, we will feel good about ourselves instead of wishing we had done something different.

I'm sure you can think of some things that would cause a lifetime of regret, but I'll list just a few. We need to understand how serious "a lifetime of regret" can be, because that should give us a lot of courage to stay away from situations that could cause it. For example:

*Getting in the car with a drunk driver.* This could hurt or even kill people. On top of that, if you were to get seriously injured, it could keep you from living the life you've always dreamed of, and it could be extremely expensive in a lot of ways for your family.

*Getting pregnant.* This would definitely change your plans. You could miss out on some important opportunities and experiences because you would have to take on a lot of grown-up responsibilities before you're ready to handle them.

*Telling a lie to a teacher to cover up for something done wrong.* If you were to get in big trouble for lying to a teacher, some people would never forget it and would not trust you again. Becoming a person of strong character is really important. Telling the truth is like an investment in good character. When people lie, they usually don't get away with one little untruth; they end up feeling they have to weave a whole big complicated web of lies to keep their story going. Just always do your best to do the right thing, and if you don't for some reason, then tell the truth about it so people will think of you as a person of integrity, not as someone who lies and cannot be trusted.

> Telling the truth is like an investment in good character.

*Losing a friendship because of gossip.* Good friendships are treasures, and gossip can be really, really hurtful. You could lose a friend for life just because you wanted to be popular and say something to the "in" crowd. When you talk about people, you affect their reputation. Sometimes, gossip follows people for the rest of their lives, and they spend years with people believing untrue things about them based on high school gossip. Would you want that to happen to you? I wouldn't. When you talk about someone, make sure it will affect that person in a positive way, not a negative way.

Don't get me wrong. I do not like awkward. I don't know anyone who does. Standing up for what we believe in is not always comfortable or easy; in fact, it's usually uncomfortable and hard. Doing the right thing often means saying no when we are under pressure to say yes or standing up for beliefs other people think are old-fashioned or uncool. If we do that, other people may make fun of us or cut us down. But that's way better than doing the wrong thing and regretting it years after we have moved on from those people.

If you are a teenager, you will probably have to deal with lots of awkward situations. Those are some of the best opportunities you will ever have to build your character and your confidence and to be a person who does the right thing. I hope you will decide today that no matter what happens, you are not going to live a life of regret and you will not do things now that will bring guilt, embarrassment, or trouble on yourself or the people you love for years to come.

> Awkward situations are some of the best opportunities to build your character and your confidence and to be a person who does the right thing.

## "WHOA. I'M DIFFERENT."

My mom has always believed travel is important. She has taught us that the world is bigger than where we live—or where anyone lives—and getting to experience other cultures and see new things can teach us a lot of valuable lessons. When I had an opportunity to travel with a Junior Olympic basketball team to Austria as a thirteen-year-old, she had no problem letting me go. She knew I was mature enough to handle that experience and believed I would learn a lot from it. Did I ever!

On that trip, I first began to realize I was different—*really* different—from lots of other people, and that was a big surprise for me. It started when I met my roommates. One was from New Jersey and one was from Maine. And there I was, from Louisiana. I don't think my roommates had any relatives with long beards or pickup trucks with shotgun racks in the windows. I'm pretty sure their dads' careers did not involve duck calls. And I'm almost positive their grandfathers did not skin frogs in the backyard! As big as those differences were, they were not the only things that set me apart from those girls.

My roommates were very similar to all the other girls on the team because they were very much "of this world." I was the only Christian in the group. None of them had been raised going to church or knowing anything about God or the Bible. One time I mentioned something about Lazarus being raised from the dead and a girl looked at me like I was crazy. I said, "You know, Lazarus? The guy in the Bible?"

She said, "No. I don't know. Never heard of him." At that time in my life, I had never been around people who were not familiar with God's Word, so that was a shock to me. I had to figure out how to deal with it, and the best way I knew was to try to show the fruit of the Spirit as I interacted with the other girls.

I was even more shocked by the way the girls behaved and by the conversations they had. I remember calling my mom and saying, "You will not *believe* what they are talking about!" My mom understood that I was around people who were not raised the way I was and did not know anything about following God, and she just encouraged me to stay true to myself and do a great job on the basketball court. And I'm sure she prayed *a lot*!

The girls on the team partied every night, but I did not want to participate in that. One of them even said to me, "You're like an old, broken-down lawn mower stuck in the garage and all of us are red Ferraris."

I did not like being called a broken-down lawn mower, but it was better than giving up my values. Even as a young teenager, I knew my family and I had worked hard to help me become a godly girl, and I was not going to sacrifice that to fit in with a group with whom I would only spend a week of my life. I knew, as a Christian, I needed to be kind and encouraging to everyone, even if they thought I was a bit weird.

My coach could tell the difference between my teammates and me. One day she said, "There is something different about you." In response, I just explained to her that I was a Christian.

Toward the end of our trip, four teams from the United States got together and chose one person to present the coach with a gift. I could hardly believe they chose me! After all the time we spent together and all the bonding experiences we had as a team, everyone knew I was different, but they did not see the difference as bad; they saw it as something they could respect.

I'm happy to say that my coach still messages me sometimes and I hear from my teammates by text or on Facebook. One of the girls even wrote me recently and said she is trying to stop cussing because she realizes it's not good. I'm really glad about that. I still talk to some of the girls sometimes and when appropriate, I send them Bible verses or other things to encourage them.

My trip to Austria and my experience on the basketball team was the first time I saw how different the world was from how I'd been raised. Before that trip, I didn't know anything about what the world is like, but I needed to find out, and I needed a chance to stand up for what I believed in. Back then, I did not really understand that believers are different from the rest of the world. We *need* to be different; that's part of what it means to follow God. I learned on that trip that just living by the fruit of the Spirit goes a long way. I had choices to make every day. I could be judgmental toward people who were not like I was, or I could try to be kind and loving. That's what I did, and it turned out really well!

## GIRL MEETS BOY, BOY MEETS GIRL

Relationships in high school can get pretty awkward. If you watch *Duck Dynasty*, you have seen John Luke and me go through some of these moments. It doesn't get any more awkward than hearing your grandfather talk about sexually transmitted diseases while stuck out in a boat on a first date, or knowing your dad is taking your boyfriend snake hunting and wondering what he could possibly be saying, or having your grandmother tell you what to do and not do on a date in front of all of your friends at the bowling alley. Yep, all those things really happened and are on television for everyone to see.

While things like this can be embarrassing in the moment, what my family has taught me most of all is not to be afraid to talk about relationships openly and freely. They just tell it like it is. My papaw Phil has been known to come straight out and ask, "Have you kissed him yet?" or say to a boy, "Keep it in your pants."

Seriously! Could it get any more awkward than that? But in the end, I appreciate it, because it brings it all out in the open. Nothing is off-limits to talk about in my family, and that gives me the courage to speak up even about things some people find awkward. Once you've discussed STDs with your grandfather, you can talk about anything!

We are all aware of the temptations that go along with a dating relationship, and not talking about them doesn't make the temptations go away. I believe being open about things from the very beginning can help in most situations, so my approach is to come right out and talk about the uncomfortable situations before they come up. As I wrote about in the chapter on respecting relationships, just put your expectations out there from day one. Make sure your boyfriend knows you are a daughter of the King and you expect to be treated as such.

The Bible tells us that our bodies are temples of the Holy Spirit. Have you ever thought about that—your body as a temple? 1 Corinthians 6:18–20 says:

*Flee from sexual immorality.*
*All other sins a person commits are outside the body,*
*but whoever sins sexually, sins against their own body.*
*Do you not know that your bodies are temples of the Holy Spirit,*
*who is in you, whom you have received from God?*
*You are not your own; you were bought at a price.*
*Therefore honor God with your bodies.*[11]

Make it your goal to stay pure and make that goal known from day one. There are ways you can help yourself do that and perhaps prevent yourself from having those five-seconds-of-awkward moments. A few ways to do this would be to lay down "rules" for yourself in your dating relationship so you don't get to that awkward moment, such as:

*Don't be home alone together.* If you and your boyfriend plan to hang out together at your house and you get home to find nobody else is there, go to the park, or go hang out at Starbucks until someone else from your family comes home. Go to a public place rather than staying home alone and perhaps opening yourself up to temptation.

*Stay out of each other's bedrooms.* Don't lie in a bed together and watch a movie or even spend time alone in each other's bedrooms together talking. Hang out with your family or watch a movie in the living room where your parents walk through every once in a while and keep you accountable.

*Pray together before each date to keep God first in your relationship.* By doing this you will remind yourselves of Whose you are and that you are living your life for Him.

Even with all of these suggestions, there is a chance you will have those five seconds of awkward in a dating relationship. If that time comes, don't be afraid to speak up and even "flee," as the Bible says. I can promise you, in the end, your boyfriend will respect you for it—that is, if you are dating the right kind of guy. And if he is not the kind of guy who respects you for that, as my uncle Jase says, "cull him" as soon as possible!

# TAKE THE FIVE-SECOND PLEDGE

I want to put out a challenge for teenagers everywhere. If you're anything like me, you really want to live a good life. You don't want to mess up a day, a week, or a year—and you definitely do not want to mess up the rest of your life by doing something now that you will regret later.

You can put the pledge I'm going to share with you on your phone, write it on your wall, tape it to your steering wheel, or stick in on your bathroom mirror. Just copy it and put it where you can see it often. Most of all, memorize it, and let it be more than words to you. Choose to let the words move out of your brain and into your heart, so they become words you live by for the rest of your life:

*I will stand up for my beliefs and I will do what's right,*
*no matter what.*
*I'll stand strong against temptation and peer pressure.*
*God has an amazing future planned for me,*
*and I won't let five seconds of awkward ruin a lifetime of awesome.*

# Live Original Challenge

1. What's the most awkward moment you've ever had?

_____

_____

_____

_____

2. In your most awkward moment, did you make a good decision or a bad one? (If you made a bad choice, even though it may have long-term consequences, you can be forgiven and redeemed. You'll always have another chance to make good decisions!)

_____

_____

_____

_____

3. When it comes to boyfriend/girlfriend stuff, what kinds of situations are most awkward for you?

_____

_____

_____

_____

4. Think about your answer to question 3. Now think about how you believe you should deal with those things. Based on what you believe, come up with a plan to help yourself say no when you need to say no or stand up for your convictions. Even if you have to write yourself a script and practice what you will say in certain situations or if you have to promise a friend or a parent you will call them if you need them, do it! If you know ahead of time what you will and will not do, you won't have to make a last-minute decision you might later regret.

_____

_____

_____

_____

_____

## DON'T FORGET

**Five seconds of awkward
can save you from a lifetime of regret!**

*"Don't worry about tomorrow,*
*for tomorrow will bring its own worries.*
*Today's trouble is enough for today."*

—Matthew 6:34

# CHAPTER TWELVE

## Stress Causes a Mess

*I*'ll admit it: I'm a worrier, and I can get really stressed out over things. Some people in my family are also worriers and some are not. I think worrying is a tendency you are born with, but it does not mean you should let it control you or take over your life. It's just something some of us have to work on more than others.

But there are others in my family who don't seem to ever worry—my mom, for instance. Any mom who will send her daughter to Austria alone at age thirteen is *not* much of a worrier. She seems to just believe things will work out, and if they don't, she will deal with them then. She is always calm in stressful situations, and I am calmer just by watching her. Two-Mama says my mom has always been that way. Even as a little girl, she was not really afraid of anything and didn't seem to worry.

John Luke inherited that carefree attitude from Mom; I did not. He and I could not be more different when it comes to worrying. For example, whenever a family member flies on an airplane, I worry about whether or not they will arrive safely at their destination. John Luke is getting his pilot's license and can hardly wait to take his first solo flight. When we were in Hawaii, I was nervous the whole time we were surfing (because, you know, there are sharks in the ocean), but John Luke has his scuba license. He would think seeing a shark would be awesome. I keep an inhaler and Benadryl with me all the time—even though I don't have allergies or asthma! John Luke—who does have allergies *and* asthma—never carries those things. (I think he knows I'm doing the worrying for him. I know, I need to work on that.) If I have to stay home alone, I check and double check to make sure all the doors are locked, and I keep an eye on the security cameras. And I'll admit, I also plan an escape route—just in case I need it to get out quickly. John Luke, on the other hand, doesn't even think about someone breaking in and just enjoys having the house to himself for a while. I don't like to drive without a GPS, while John Luke actually refuses to use anything to help him know where he's going because it would ruin the sense of adventure.

> God must know that a lot of people worry, or He wouldn't have put so many instructions about not doing it in the Bible!

I am trying to overcome my tendency to worry so much. I have reached the point where I can laugh about it. In fact, I wrote something about it, just to poke fun at myself:

When I think ocean, I think shark.

When I think plane, I think crash.

When I think headache, I think brain cancer.

When I think home alone, I think kidnapped.

When I think "unknown number," I think *Taken*.

When I think cough, I think asthma.

When I think quiet, I think "they must not like me."

When I think tubing, I think snake.

When I think motorcycle, I think death.

As I said, I really am working to overcome my tendency to worry because I have figured out that worry can take away my joy and fun. Besides that, the Bible is full of verses that tell people not to worry or stress or be afraid, so living a worry-free life must be important to God. He must know that a lot of people worry, or He wouldn't have put so many instructions about not doing it in the Bible! He knows we need to be reminded to stay calm and be at peace because that's the way we can live our best lives.

# A BLUE NEVUS?

Have you ever heard of a blue nevus (pronounced like "leave us," with an "n" instead of an "l")? I had not, until three doctors told me they thought I had one. Here's how the story unfolded.

One day, I had my feet up and Two-Mama noticed a spot on one of them. It was kind of dark blue, in the shape of a dot. I had not seen it before, but I got a little worried after she asked me about it. A few days later, I was at a friend's house. Her father is a doctor, so I showed it to him. "Hmmmm," he said, "that looks like a blue nevus. You better have someone check it out further."

So I showed it to another friend's father, also a doctor. "That looks like a blue nevus or some kind of skin cancer," he told me. "You need to see a dermatologist about that."

I had no idea what a blue nevus was, but after two doctors encouraged me to investigate it—and the second one mentioned skin cancer—I got pretty nervous. By the time I saw my dermatologist, I was really worried.

"Yep, that definitely looks like a blue nevus. We need to take a biopsy of it," she said after looking at the spot. By that time, I was almost in total fear and panic, completely stressed out about it.

The dermatologist got some kind of tool to use for the biopsy and started scraping the blue place—and the whole thing came right off! It wasn't a blue nevus, after all. It was an ink spot! I had stepped in some ink about a week earlier at camp, when we were tie-dying T-shirts, so it was the kind of ink that does not come off easily with soap and water. I was fine, and everyone got a good laugh when it was over.

Another time, not long after the mystery of the blue nevus was solved, I got really scared because I started having headaches and my vision got blurry for about a week. At that time, I was trying not to be such a worrier, so I did not mention this to anyone. About a week later, I started getting nosebleeds and ended up with a red ring under my eye on the same side of my face where the nosebleeds were happening, so I finally told my mom. I was really worried that something terrible was wrong with me. As it turned out, I just needed glasses and the nosebleed and ring under my eye just happened because my springtime allergies were acting up—totally unrelated.

The important lesson I learned from these experiences is not to get all worried and upset about things until you know the facts. I spent a lot of time worrying about an ink spot on my foot, afraid it was something really serious when it wasn't. I could have used that time to have fun, to think positively, or to do something for someone else instead of being self-focused and worried. Things often turn out better than we think they will. We just need to resist the temptation to worry and choose to believe the best about our circumstances, knowing God will see us through them.

# STRESS STARTS WITH WORRY

The title of this chapter is pretty catchy, don't you think? I mean, I've got the rhyme going on and everything—*stress causes a mess!* But it's true. Stress causes major problems, and stress often starts with worry. Actually, the words "stress" and "worry" basically describe the same thing—being really anxious about something. As teenagers we don't usually think much about making choices for our long-term health. We may see our parents or grandparents making choices to exercise more, lose weight, or eat better so they can become healthier, or we may know someone who has been sick and is now on a special diet, like low sugar or low salt (which doesn't sound very good to me). Many of these people will tell you they wish they had made healthier choices when they were younger. Some of their doctors would even say that their health problems are related to not handling stress very well over the years. So I'm thinking you and I better start now to learn how to deal with stress and worry. That way, we can stay healthy for a lifetime.

High school and even junior high are great places to learn to manage stress, because there's a lot of stress in those places. Think about it: we have to balance classes, homework, pop quizzes, exams, extracurricular activities, friends, family, church, learning to drive, bad hair days, and boyfriend-girlfriend relationships—and even hormones—all at the same time. No wonder we're stressed!

If you walk down the halls of any high school, you will probably hear someone talking about being stressed over a test, a sports tryout, a play or band audition, a relationship, or something. What they really mean is that they are worried about those things. We get stressed because we are worried that we won't pass the test, won't make the team, won't get a role in the play or a place in the band, or might lose whoever we think is the current love of our life. As I mentioned, worry leads to stress, and stress is a really bad thing.

> I'm thinking you and I better start now to learn how to deal with stress and worry.

There's a famous place called the Mayo Clinic, and on their website, they list some of the negative ways stress can affect us and some things it can cause, including: headache, stomach upset, sleep problems, anxiety, lack of motivation, inability to focus or concentrate, feeling depressed, overeating or undereating, drug or alcohol use, angry outbursts, and withdrawing from other people.[12] Not good!

Stress is bad for us, bad for the things we want to accomplish, and bad for our relationships. But there is a better way.

## NO WORRY, NO STRESS, NO FEAR

In chapter 3, I wrote about my mom's grandparents Alton and Jean Howard, and I mentioned that Mamaw Howard was known for being a prayer warrior and a woman of great faith. One of the greatest gifts she left our family was her love for the Bible. She quoted Bible verses all the time.

On my phone, I have a video of Mamaw Howard quoting her favorite Bible verse, Isaiah 41:10, in the old King James Version, with all the "thee"s and "thou"s and "yea"s. My cousins and I can all quote this verse in the King James Version because we heard Mamaw say it so many times. The truth of these words was so real and important to her that she wanted to make sure all of us knew it too. We did not totally appreciate her efforts when we were children, but we do now.

Like a lot of people in Louisiana, Mamaw Howard had a very strong southern accent. She could stretch out a word like "my" for two or three syllables and emphasize it like it was the most important word in the English language, especially when she said, "I will uphold thee with the right hand of *my* righteousness." Anyone who ever heard her quote the scripture could tell she believed it with all her heart.

In my favorite version of the Bible, the New Living Translation, this verse says,

> *Don't be afraid, for I am with you.*
> *Don't be discouraged, for I am your God.*
> *I will strengthen you and help you.*
> *I will hold you up with my victorious right hand.*

No matter which version you read it in, the message is the same: "Don't worry. God will take care of you." If we really believe that, we will stay calm and trust Him, no matter what happens.

# GOD'S GOT IT

I can understand why people worry about certain things. I've already said I have a tendency to worry too. One thing that is just true about life is that there will always be something—big or small—that we can worry about if we want to. The opposite is also true. If we don't want to worry, we don't have to. We can choose instead to do what Jesus teaches us to do in Matthew 6:25–27:

*"That is why I tell you not to worry about everyday life—*
*whether you have enough food and drink,*
*or enough clothes to wear.*
*Isn't life more than food, and your body more than clothing?*
*Look at the birds. They don't plant or harvest or store food in barns,*
*for your heavenly Father feeds them.*
*And aren't you far more valuable to him than they are?*
*Can all your worries add a single moment to your life?"*

Jesus asks a great question, one all of us need to think about: "Can all your worries add a single moment to your life?" In other words, can worrying help anything or change anything? That's a big no. If worry won't change things, why do we spend our time doing it?

A Dutch lady named Corrie Ten Boom lived a pretty dramatic life during World War II and wrote a book about her experiences called *The Hiding Place*. After the war started, she had lots of good reasons to worry. Her family helped hide Jewish people when the Germans were trying to send them to concentration camps. During the war, Corrie and her family were captured, and they ended up in a concentration camp because they had helped the Jews. Some of her family members died in the camps, but Corrie survived, was released, and came to live in the United

> "Worry does not empty tomorrow of its sorrow. It empties today of its strength."
> —Corrie Ten Boom

States. She said, "Worry does not empty tomorrow of its sorrow. It empties today of its strength." That is so true, and I'm sure she must have learned it the hard way.

If you are anything like I am, you want to live today the best you can. You definitely do not want to rob today of its strength, because you need that strength to do what you're supposed to do, to stand up for what you believe in, to be a good friend and family member, to do well in school, and to go after your dreams. Next time you are tempted to worry, remember that it will not change anything about the future, but it will steal the energy you need for today.

A lot of people say their favorite Bible verse is Jeremiah 29:11, where God says,

> For I know the plans I have for you . . .
> They are plans for good and not for disaster,
> to give you a future and a hope.

Is there any reason to worry when God has good plans for you? I don't think so!

## INSTEAD OF WORRYING, YOU COULD DO THIS

Trying to overcome worry all by yourself can be pretty hard. The best way I know to overcome it is to ask God to help us. He actually tells us to lay all our burdens on Him, and it's amazing what He will do for us if we just ask.

The apostle Paul wrote several of the books in the New Testament. He went through a *lot* in his life, and the books he wrote (which are really letters to different groups or individuals) are full of great lessons and advice about how to live. If you are not very familiar with the Bible and want to start reading it, Paul's writings would be a great place to start. Some of the books he wrote, like Philippians and Colossians, are just a few chapters long, so you could read them pretty quickly.

Paul had been shipwrecked, thrown in jail, and persecuted. I'm pretty sure there were many times in his life he could have worried. Instead, he wrote:

> *Don't worry about anything; instead, pray about everything.*
> *Tell God what you need, and thank him for all he has done.*
> *Then you will experience God's peace,*
> *which exceeds anything we can understand.*
> *His peace will guard your hearts and minds*
> *as you live in Christ Jesus.*
> —Philippians 4:6–7

This is exactly what we need to do when we start to worry. We need to tell ourselves to stop worrying and start praying. As Paul says, that's the way to experience God's peace. And peace is the total opposite of stress.

## HOW TO FIGHT STRESS

Sometimes, just reading a book that tells you not to worry is not enough. You need to know what to do with your mind when it gets tempted to worry. When your brain starts getting afraid or stressed about something, it's hard to just shut down those thoughts. If you can replace them with other thoughts, that helps a lot. The thoughts I'm going to suggest you replace your stress with all come from God's Word.

As I end this chapter, I want to share ten scriptures that can become your weapons against worry and stress.

> When your brain starts getting afraid or stressed, it's hard to just shut down those thoughts. If you can replace them with other thoughts, that helps a lot.

Some of them are short enough to memorize pretty quickly. You can put these verses in your phone or on a piece of paper so you can find them easily. Then, when you start to get anxious about something, you can look at them and fill your mind with them, so you can begin to overcome your worries and fears.

### 1
*"Be strong and courageous!*
*Do not be afraid and do not panic before them.*
*For the Lord your God will personally go ahead of you.*
*He will neither fail you nor abandon you."*
—Deuteronomy 31:6

This is a perfect verse to read when you are starting something new—like going to a new school or going to summer camp for the first time, or even when something bigger is happening, like you're moving across the country or your mom is getting remarried and you have to get to know a stepbrother or stepsister. Don't you feel relieved to know God is going ahead of you? I also love the last part of this verse. People are going to disappoint you at some point, they may even abandon you, but God will *never* fail you or abandon you. That should give you some peace right there!

### 2
*I prayed to the Lord, and he answered me.*
*He freed me from all my fears.*
*Those who look to him for help will be radiant with joy;*
*no shadow of shame will darken their faces.*
*In my desperation I prayed, and the Lord listened;*
*he saved me from all my troubles.*
—Psalm 34:4–6

This passage is great for when you are afraid. I used to be afraid of thunderstorms. I'm happy to say God has freed me from that fear, and He can free you from whatever you are afraid of too.

### 3

*God is our refuge and strength,*
*always ready to help in times of trouble.*
—Psalm 46:1

Memorize this one when you are going through a tough time— like maybe when someone close to you passes away or your parents are going through a divorce. Know that through the trouble God is always there. He is there for you as your safe place, and you can lean on Him for strength.

### 4

*Give your burdens to the Lord,*
*and he will take care of you.*
*He will not permit the godly to slip and fall.*
—Psalm 55:22

This verse can encourage you when you are stressed because there is too much on your plate. Maybe you feel pressure to make cheerleading or get straight As and you feel the burden of all the pressures of high school. Know that God will take care of you and will hold you up.

### 5

*But when I am afraid, I will put my trust in you.*
—Psalm 56:3

Another good one for when you are afraid. This is a statement: I *will* put my trust in you. Memorize it. Just saying it makes you feel better.

### 6

*Then Jesus said, "Come to me,*
*all of you who are weary and carry heavy burdens,*
*and I will give you rest.*
*Take my yoke upon you.*
*Let me teach you, because I am humble and gentle at heart,*
*and you will find rest for your souls.*
*For my yoke is easy to bear, and the burden I give you is light."*
—Matthew 11:28–30

You don't have to do *anything* on your own. You don't have to handle it all. Jesus wants to take your burdens from you. He's even talking about the "heavy burdens." The tough stuff. We go through some hard things on this earth, and Jesus says He can handle it all. He also tells us He is humble and gentle. People don't always handle the burdens we give them very gently. Some people are downright harsh or mean. When you give something to God, He will handle it gently and will give you rest. This is good news!

### 7

*"I am leaving you with a gift—peace of mind and heart.*
*And the peace I give is a gift the world cannot give.*
*So don't be troubled or afraid."*
—John 14:27

The kind of peace God gives is much greater than anything in this world. He is the kind of Father who loves to give good gifts to His children. That's something no amount of money can buy.

## 8

*Letting your sinful nature control your mind leads to death.*
*But letting the Spirit control your mind leads to life and peace.*
—Romans 8:6

If we put our faith and trust in God and allow His Spirit to work within us, we will have peace. If we don't have peace, we should examine ourselves and make sure we are living the kind of life God calls us to live. When we live godly lives, even though things will not be perfect, we can have peace through the imperfections.

## 9

*If God is for us, who can ever be against us?*
—Romans 8:31

This is a great verse for times when you feel like friends are turning against you or people at school are spreading gossip about you, or maybe you have a teacher who just seems to have it out for you. God's got your back!

## 10

*Give all your worries and cares to God,*
*for he cares about you.*
—1 Peter 5:7

God *loves* you! He cares about you. He is willing to take all of your worries. We just have to give them to Him. I love the *Veggie-Tales* song that says God is bigger than the Boogie Man. It's a really cute little tune that basically lets us know there is nothing God can't handle and no way He is ever going to leave us or fail to take care of us. He is always watching out for us.

I know it sometimes feels like there's a lot to get anxious or upset about, but don't let worry and stress cause a mess in your life. God's bigger than all of that, and He is *seriously* on your side!

# Live Original Challenge

1. Have you ever let your mind run away with worry and then had everything turn out okay in the end? How did that make you feel?

_____

_____

_____

2. Why is it important to get all the facts before you jump to a conclusion about something and get worried or upset about it?

_____

_____

_____

3. Jeremiah 29:11 says God has good plans for your future. Next time you worry about what's ahead, how can this verse help you not stress?

_____

_____

_____

4. Of the Bible verses listed in this chapter to help you overcome worry, which one will you choose to memorize so it can help you stay calm and peaceful?

_____

_____

## DON'T FORGET

**Don't worry.
God will help you and take care of you!**

*What good is it, dear brothers and sisters,*
*if you say you have faith but don't show it by your actions?*
*Can that kind of faith save anyone?*
*Suppose you see a brother or sister who has no food or clothing,*
*and you say, "Good-bye and have a good day;*
*stay warm and eat well"*
*—but then you don't give that person any food or clothing.*
*What good does that do? So you see, faith by itself isn't enough.*
*Unless it produces good deeds, it is dead and useless.*

—James 2:14–17

## CHAPTER THIRTEEN

# Do Something

One of my favorite quotes is: "Be the change you want to see in the world." In other words, when you see something that needs to be different, do something about it. You could think about what's wrong with the world; you could even talk about it, read about it, and have discussions with your friends about how it needs to change. But if you really want things to change, you have to do something.

As teenagers, we don't always think we are old enough to make a difference in the world. That is just not true. I want to share some true stories of very young children who have made a major impact on the world because they realized something needed to change. And then there's the teenager whose personal diary from the 1940s still gets read today. Check these out.

- Alexandra "Alex" Scott was diagnosed with cancer before she was even a year old. At age four, she told her parents she wanted to raise money to help find a cure for cancer. So she set up a lemonade stand—and, with her brother, raised more than $2,000 in one day. After

Alex passed away at the age of eight, her parents continued her efforts. Since 2005, Alex's Lemonade Stand Foundation has raised more than seventy-five million dollars to fight cancer and help people affected by it.

• Blare Gooch cried when he saw a photo of a little boy in a pile of rubble after the 2010 earthquake in Haiti, and he wished the little boy could have a teddy bear. So Blare did something about it. He started asking people at his school to donate bears; they did, and then many others started giving bears too. He eventually sent twenty-five thousand teddy bears to Haiti and about twenty-two thousand to other nonprofit organizations. He said, "It doesn't really matter how small or old you are. If you're young and think you can't make a difference in the world, well, you actually can."[13]

• Think about the Jewish teenager named Anne Frank. You may have read her book, *The Diary of a Young Girl*. Even though she died in 1945, in a concentration camp, when she was only fifteen years old, a *lot* of people have read this book. It has sold millions and millions of copies and been printed in more than fifty languages. When people read *The Diary of a Young Girl*, they remember what happened to the Jews during World War II. Because of her diary, this young girl has kept a very important time in history from getting lost or overlooked.

Alex Scott, Blare Gooch, and Anne Frank were all young, but they had huge impacts on the world. In their own way, they each did something about situations that needed to change. For Alex, it was raising money to find a cure for cancer. For Blare, it was collecting teddy bears to comfort children who had lost everything. For Anne, it was writing her thoughts and experiences in a diary people would read for generations. No matter how young—or old—you are, you can do something to change the world.

> No matter how young—or old—you are, you can do something to change the world.

# IT'S ALL ABOUT ACTION

John Luke has a T-shirt that says, "Don't say you're going to do it, do it." Seriously, people could talk for years about what they want to do, but unless and until they take action, everything stays the same. I love Matthew West's song "Do Something." That song tells the story of someone thinking about the trouble in the world and wondering why God doesn't do something about it—and then the person realizes God did do something: He created you and me. We can be God's hands and feet. Maybe He doesn't reach down from heaven in some dramatic way and make everything that's wrong right, but He created us, and He expects us to do something. He works through us to see what needs changing and to act on it.

One time, my boyfriend said to me, "I wish my school was more spiritual, like yours is."

Instead of saying, "Yeah, it's too bad your school isn't more spiritual. I'm really sorry about that," I said, "What are you going to do about it?"

I knew he could change the situation if he wanted to.

This is one reason I wrote the chapter "You Can Only Fix You." If every person can understand how we can start with ourselves and then change the world around us, amazing things can happen. I hope that the tools and suggestions in this book are helpful, but don't just read the book, go out and live the book.

You might be thinking, *I am just a teenager, I've got my whole life ahead of me. I'll do something to change the world when I'm older.*

But I'm thinking, *You're a teenager! What better time to make a difference! How great is it that you don't have to wait until you finish college or have a job or get married to start to change things?*

You only live once. You have only one chance to make your mark on this world. If you miss an opportunity to change things today, that opportunity is gone forever. So take advantage of who you are right now. Make the most of the opportunities right in front of you. Take advantage of the way you see the world, with your unique point of view, and use your energy and passion to make a difference. Don't just notice or talk about what's wrong in the world, do something to make it better.

# THE PEOPLE WHO CHANGED MY WORLD

I have learned firsthand what a difference just doing something can make in the lives of other people and in my own life. When I was eleven years old, Two-Mama took me on my first mission trip. She had taken John Luke the year before, and I got to go with them the next year. We went to a city called Neiba (pronounced "Nay-buh") in the Dominican Republic, and it changed my life. In fact, I have been going on the mission trip to this place every summer since, and it's one of my all-time very favorite things to do.

This trip is not something we decided to do after *Duck Dynasty* started; it's something people in our family have done for years. In fact, the people we know in Neiba had never heard of the Robertsons until just recently. We shared some Spanish episodes of our show with them, and they think seeing us on TV is really fun. But the fact that we are on television is not a big deal to them. They were sweet, kind, and affectionate to us before they knew about the show—just as they were to all the volunteers who visited them. Now that they've seen the show, the way they treat us hasn't changed at all. We like that. We are not interested in being celebrities to them, we are only interested in doing what we can to help them, meet their needs, and share God's love when we are with them.

Our church found out about the needs of Neiba through World Radio (the international ministry my great-grandfather started). Poverty is a big problem there, so that's where they decided to go.

Now most of our family goes to Neiba every year. We really fell in love with the children at the orphanage there. One of the coolest things about our relationships with them is that we are getting to watch them grow up. We send them presents and things at Christmastime, but we only visit them once a year, and we are so excited when that time finally rolls around every summer. When we are not with them, we miss them—they have become like part of the family. Thankfully, social media makes it easier to keep in touch with them, but that is a little challenging because they do not speak much English. Some of the older boys do know the word "hey," so we sometimes have whole conversations with them by just saying "hey" back and forth several times. Even though we only hear that one word, being in touch with them makes us happy, and I hope it helps them remember that we love them and care about them.

Before my first trip, I thought I was going to go to this faraway place, see true poverty for the first time, and make the people so happy. I hope I made them happy, but the surprise was that I was the one who was made happy. I could hardly stop smiling because I realized in a new way that things do not make people happy; happiness comes from the inside. Our friends in Neiba do not have much at all in terms of worldly possessions, but they have so much joy and love.

> I hope I made them happy, but the surprise was that I was the one who was made happy.

# LITTLE THINGS MEAN A LOT

One person who means a lot to me is a little girl named Maria. As I'm writing this book, she is about twelve years old and lives in the orphanage. When we got to Neiba in the summer of 2013, we noticed that the mattress on her bed was not straight and firm, like it should have been. It was lumpy and sunken, as though it had no supports under it.

One day, Maria and I were outside playing. She was so happy that day, and I was happy just to be with her. While we played, my mom and some others from our group went to a store and got Maria a whole new bed. They moved out the old one and moved in the new one in a pretty short amount of time.

When we went inside, Maria saw her new bed. We will never forget the look of total happiness and surprise on her face. She fell to the ground in tears. She was bawling, and all her tears were tears of joy. I had never seen such pure, overwhelmed emotion. She was so grateful!

That day, I realized I have never received a gift that totally overwhelmed me and brought me to tears. In my country, a lot of people have nice beds. For most American kids, a bed is something their parents provide for them, not something that would be considered a gift. But for Maria, the new bed was one of the best gifts we could have given her. She appreciated it so much, but I think she appreciated even more the fact that we loved her enough to give it to her. Seeing her so happy made us happy too.

# WHAT ARE YOU WAITING FOR?

I got my passport when I was eleven years old, before my first trip to the Dominican Republic. I definitely look eleven in the photo, braces and all. I'm glad I got the passport when I was so young and was able to travel overseas to do mission work at an early age because of the difference it has made in my life.

A mission trip is a great way to do something to change the world, and while you're at it, your life will be changed too. I encourage everyone I meet to take one of these trips. Maybe your church takes a mission trip every summer, or if not, maybe you could go with some friends through their church. In addition, there are several mission ministries that offer trips for teenagers and young adults. Doing something like this might only take one week out of your summer vacation, but it could be the best week of your whole life. Or you might end up like I have, visiting the same group of people every year and really getting to know them, love them, and watch them grow up.

I don't think there is anything as good for a teenager as a mission trip. That kind of experience usually makes people more grateful and selfless. It gives an up-close look at poverty and real need, and it teaches us how really blessed we are. More than that, it reminds us that money cannot buy love or happiness and gives us an opportunity to love others in new and selfless ways. It teaches us that part of our responsibility as Christians is to care for people who do not have as much as we do.

One lesson I have learned on my mission trips is that I do not need all the food and conveniences I have in the U.S. In the Dominican Republic, we eat beans and rice for a whole week. We do not have hot water or air-conditioning. But we don't complain (that wouldn't change anything); most of the time we are having so much fun and are so amazed by the people we meet that we don't even think about hot water.

We also learn to share, even when we don't think we have "much" the way we usually think about "much." (We always have much, compared to our friends in Neiba.) Think about it. We have smartphones; they do not even have clean water. In fact, the water in their community is so bad the locals don't even drink it. We take bottled water to share with them, and where an American might drink three-fourths of a bottle and throw away the rest, they will beg for the little bit that's left and drink it with gratitude. They even think a breath mint is a treat! I've become a much more grateful person since I've been going on mission trips, and I think that has made me a better Christian and a more loving person.

I love the freedom and joy the people in Neiba live with. They really do not care what anyone thinks of them, especially when it comes to praying or praising God. They have so much love for Him and so much faith. When they sing, we might think it's off key, but it's awesome because it's so passionate and sincere. They sing praises to God with all their hearts, and that's what makes it beautiful.

Are you excited yet? Are you starting to want to go on a mission trip? I really encourage you to think and pray about doing it—and to go get a passport, just in case God leads you to take this kind of adventure, you're ready. Yep, I'm talking to you!

# YOU DON'T HAVE TO GO FAR

I know. I get really excited about encouraging people to take mission trips overseas. But I also understand that not everyone can travel to another country. Sometimes I take mission trips to places as close to where I live as Alabama, or even in our own city. Local mission opportunities are great too. I get to serve in some of the same ways whether I'm in Neiba or somewhere near my home. If people can travel out of the country, that's great. But mission fields are everywhere. You do not have to go around the world to find one. You might actually have one practically in your own backyard.

> You do not have to go around the world to find a mission field. You might actually have one practically in your own backyard.

Not long ago, I had a basketball tournament game at a school about an hour and a half from West Monroe. Looking at the places we passed as my family and I drove there, I thought, *This looks like the Dominican Republic*. That's the kind of poverty I saw—and I didn't have to pack a suitcase or get a passport stamped to see it. It was actually pretty close to home.

No doubt, you have a mission field close to you too. It might not be a place where people do not have much money; it might be an elderly neighbor who lacks company and would enjoy a conversation with you. It might not be an orphanage full of children over-seas; it might be your younger siblings, cousins, or neighbors who need you to be a good role model and to encourage them.

My mission trip experiences changed my whole way of looking at life. I am thankful for that. Whether your mission field is across the street or around the world, I hope you will step out of your comfort zone and do something to help people and make a differ-ence in the world. If something needs to change, you can make it happen.

# Live Original Challenge

1. What change do you want to see in the world?

_____

_____

_____

_____

2. What specific thing can you do to be the change you want to see?

_____

_____

_____

3. Have you ever done something really nice for someone who could not do it for himself or herself? How did that make you feel?

_____

_____

_____

4. How can you help people in your own neighborhood, city, or state?

_____

_____

_____

## DON'T FORGET

**"Be the change you want to see in the world."**
**Do something!**

*You made all the delicate, inner parts of my body*
*and knit me together in my mother's womb.*
*Thank you for making me so wonderfully complex!*
*Your workmanship is marvelous—how well I know it.*
*You watched me as I was being formed in utter seclusion,*
*as I was woven together in the dark of the womb.*
*You saw me before I was born.*
*Every day of my life was recorded in your book.*
*Every moment was laid out*
*before a single day had passed.*

—Psalm 139:13–16

## CHAPTER FOURTEEN

# Live Original

When people tell stories about me from when I was really little, I just have to trust them. I mean, I definitely do not remember everything I did when I was a preschooler. In a lot of cases, someone in our family has videos that show me doing or saying funny things when I was four or five years old—back when people thought I was really cute because I couldn't say my "R"s. For other situations, I just have to rely on people who are older than I am and remember what happened.

My mom says I was hilarious when I was little because I would imitate other people in the family. Just try to imagine it: young Sadie imitating Papaw Phil or Mamaw Kay. Apparently, I was pretty good at it!

I was also really good at telling knock-knock jokes. My favorite was:

"Knock-knock?"

"Who's there?"

"Boo."

"Boo who?"

"Don't cry. It's just a joke."

I thought that was hilarious, and my family played along like it was funny the hundredth time I said it.

I also dressed up in all kinds of costumes and sang and danced or did whatever performance I could think of that day. If I had an audience, I was happy to perform, and I had no problem putting everything out there—whether I was "preaching" on the video about God when I was five years old or doing something else. Okay, maybe I was kind of a weird child, but at least I entertained myself and kept my family laughing.

As a result of those things, when my dad would talk about me, he started saying, "She's an original." I guess he meant he had never seen another little girl who did and said the things I did, that I was one of a kind. So he started calling me "the Original." When Bella was born, he called me "the Original Big Sister."

So in a way, I've been an original all my life. I have never wanted to copy anyone else; I've always wanted to just be the best me I can be. When I was young, I did not understand the importance of being who I am and not trying to be like other people. As I've gotten older, I understand it better—and I am more determined than ever to keep living original. One of the sayings I live my life by is: "In a world that dares you to be different, be yourself." I hope you will do that too.

# BE ORIGINAL

In Merriam-Webster's online dictionary, one of the definitions of *original* is: "a person who is different from other people in an appealing or interesting way."[14] Truly, we are all originals. We all have things about our personalities and about who we are that are different, interesting, and appealing to others. God made each one of us unique. No two fingerprints are exactly alike. Think about that! It's really amazing. Even identical twins have different fingerprints and personality traits that make them unique.

There has never been nor ever will be anyone on this earth exactly like you! God took the time to design everything about you, just the way you are. You are an original created by God, and He does not make mistakes. For me, being original is really just about being your own person and being confident in who you are. It means knowing God made you in a unique way, for a unique purpose. That's something the world needs to see!

Have you ever thought of yourself as original? I hope you have, but some people haven't. They are so busy trying to fit in that they don't want to do anything to make themselves stand out. I get that; there's a lot of peer pressure in school, and almost everyone wants to be accepted. I just happen to think a person can be accepted without being a copycat. It's okay to express yourself and be bold about what you like and what you do not like—whether that has to do with fashion and appearance, hobbies and interests, or values and beliefs.

If you want to live original but are not exactly sure how to do it, here are a few questions to help you get started:

> I just happen to think a person can be accepted without being a copycat.

1. What's your very favorite thing to do?

2. What's your favorite color?

3. What's the best feature of your personality?

4. What do you do really well?

5. What dreams do you have for your future?

6. Who are your favorite people to be around?

7. Who are your role models?

8. What inspires you?

9. What character traits are most important to you?

10. What values and beliefs are most important to you?

11. If you could do one thing to change the world, what would it be?

12. If you could spend today anywhere in the world, doing anything you want, where would you be and what would you do?

As you answer these questions, you will start to see some unique things about yourself. Identifying these simple things is an easy way to start figuring out who you are, what you like, and what matters to you. Making the most of any of these things—being proud of them and not trying to hide them—will help you express who you are. Figure out what makes you an original, and do something with it.

It's also important to see the best in other people, because people do not always see the best in themselves. Sometimes it's not easy to find something good about some people, but it can be done—and you can be a person who does it. Everyone appreciates people who see the good in them instead of pointing out what's wrong with them.

Once you learn to be an original, take the challenge to help someone else do the same. It's just amazing how many different gifts and abilities and cool things are in each person, but sometimes people need a little help bringing those things out. If you are willing to do that, it will make you feel great about yourself while helping someone else feel great about him- or herself too.

# TAKE THE PRESSURE OFF

In the world, there's a lot of pressure to be like other people. Sometimes I don't think those "other people" are the best role models, but because they are "popular" or "cool," people compare themselves to them or want to be like them. I think this is really sad. When people try to find their confidence or self-worth based on whether or not they are like others, they will usually end up disappointed.

For some reason, this is a real problem among teenagers. Maybe that is because so many of us are trying to discover who we are, why we are here on earth, and what we are supposed to do with our lives. Some people do not have parents who help them grow up, and they kind of have to figure out life on their own. I can see why they could be tempted to imitate friends, celebrities, or people their age who seem to have everything together or seem interesting.

Another reason we compare ourselves to others or try to be like them is that we don't want to be rejected or feel alone. Let's face it: we all want to have friends and to be accepted. There's nothing wrong with that. God made us to want relationships. But if that desire causes us to ignore the best things about ourselves and instead try to be like other people, then we have a problem.

In our family, I don't think anyone feels pressure to be someone they're not. We are pretty good at accepting each other for who we are. We celebrate the things people do well and try to help them with what they may not do so well. Our family has always had the attitude that not everyone has to be good at everything. Everyone has strengths and weaknesses; people are good at different things. For example, John Luke is really smart, but he can't sing, and he has not exactly excelled in sports. In fact, he says, "Sadie and Will have ninety-nine percent of the athletic ability in our family—and Bella and I share the remaining one percent!"

He does not complain or feel bad about what he cannot do. He cheers me on when I play sports, he puts a lot of energy into the things he is good at, and he has a good sense of humor about the things he doesn't do so well.

Not long ago my brother Will mentioned that he does not think he is as funny as other boys in his class are. My mom said, "I think you are funny, but you may not be as funny as someone else, and that's okay. You may not be the funniest person, but you are really good at music and you are a great friend." She let him know that if we compare ourselves to others, we will always feel we come up short. There will always be someone funnier or smarter, or more athletic than we are. We have to look at the gifts God gives us and not worry about being the best at everything.

My mom says telling children and teenagers they are the best at everything is not good for them. She thinks it's much better to say, "You are great at some things but not at others. Look at the talents God gave you, and know what you're good at."

> If we compare ourselves to others, we will always feel we come up short.

Too often, especially as teenagers, we stress over not being able to do things other people can do. We look at others and compare ourselves to them when we really just need to look to God and ask if we are living like He wants us to. We get depressed about what we can't do or what we don't have, when we really need to focus on and make the most of what we do have. The Bible says it like this in Romans 12:6–8:

> *In His grace, God has given us different gifts*
> *for doing certain things well.*

*So if God has given you the ability to prophesy,*
*speak out with as much faith as God has given you.*
*If your gift is serving others, serve them well.*
*If you are a teacher, teach well.*
*If your gift is to encourage others, be encouraging.*
*If it is giving, give generously.*
*If God has given you leadership ability,*
*take the responsibility seriously.*
*And if you have a gift for showing kindness*
*to others, do it gladly.*

If we all had the same gift, we would not get much done. And let's face it: if we were all the same, life would be pretty boring. God made us all different. He gave us different gifts so we can work together to do some awesome things. What is the gift God has given you? Examine your life. Figure it out. Use that gift to help others in service to God. And don't spend another second wishing you could be like someone else.

# A GREAT OPPORTUNITY

Until I got into high school, I never thought much about prom dresses. I guess I thought I would have a couple of prom dresses in my lifetime, but I never expected to end up having my own line of dresses and getting to model them during Fashion Week in New York. But one summer, within just a few weeks, two prom dress companies contacted me about being one of their celebrities.

I appreciated both offers, but I really wanted to work with Sherri Hill's company, probably the biggest prom dress designer in

America. I was excited about doing this, not just because it was a great opportunity, but also because I saw it as a chance to do something that could make a difference. I had the idea to create a line of dresses that were "Daddy approved." Over the past several years, prom dresses have become more and more immodest—some are totally shocking. I'm not surprised Dads would be nervous about them. I was not looking to create a line of floor-length, turtleneck, denim dresses; I just knew there could be something in between that and the super-revealing dresses—dresses that would be beautiful and that girls would want to wear, but also dresses dads would be proud for their daughters to walk out the door in on prom night. I hope that doing this and speaking up about modesty will make dressing modestly cool again. After all, modest is hottest!

When the time came for me to create the collection, my mom, Two-Mama, Rebecca, Bella, and I flew from our mission trip in the Dominican Republic to Austin, Texas, where Sherri Hill's headquarters is located, and we really clicked with the people there. When the time came for me to choose the dresses for my Live Original collection, we went into a huge warehouse filled with dresses—seriously, thousands and thousands of dresses. I had never seen anything like it!

My job was to choose fifteen dresses to serve as models for the Live Original line. Once I finally narrowed them down, which was really hard, I had a chance to make changes to them. I suggested things like making hemlines longer, making tops less low-cut, or changing colors.

When the dresses were finished and the time came for me to do the photo shoot for the line, Sherri gave me a pair of Converse high tops to wear with one of them. I loved that. It was such a great visual for the whole idea of living original, and it captured so much of who I am. I like to get dressed up and have my hair, nails, and makeup done, but I'm also really casual, fun, and a little unpredictable sometimes—like tennis shoes with a prom dress.

Maybe you are the type of person who would want to wear brightly colored high tops with a nice dress, or maybe something totally different, but just as quirky, would be more your style. The point is to find out who you are and express it in every way you can. Clothes are a place to start, but you can also express yourself in lots of other ways—like the way you decorate your room or through art, music, or dance, or through the way you live your beliefs and uphold your standards.

Everything you do and say sends a message about who you are, so make sure the message represents you well!

## SURPRISE!

I love to surprise people. A surprise might be as simple as making a funny face at an unexpected time or picking up a favorite dessert from a local restaurant and taking it home to my family. But one of my favorite ways to surprise people is to do what I call my "God thing" when dealing with the media.

When a popular magazine for teen girls interviewed me about my prom dress line, I don't think they thought I would use that opportunity to talk about my faith or my values. I can't speak for them, but I think they expected me to be a teenage girl obsessing over prom and dresses and boys, and it seemed like they tried to get me to go in that direction. I was not intimidated at all. I just started talking about the importance of modesty and how great it is that the fashion world now offers dresses a dad can be proud of. I went on to share a few things about how excited I was to see dresses that are not suggestive and about how prom should be a fun time for high schoolers, not something more.

The person who interviewed me seemed caught off guard, because all she really said in response to my comments was, "Okay."

The fact is, there are non-Christian people in the world who really want to see Christians mess up or even deliberately try to get us to say or do things that will make us look like we are not serious or genuine about our faith. I am out to prove these people wrong. I'm committed to practicing what I preach—and I know, I preach a lot!

Someone asked me one time if I have always been spunky and bold enough to stand up for what I believe. The answer is yes. I'm certainly not perfect—I sin and make mistakes like anyone else—but I have always been proud of the fact that I am a Christian. I'm not one of those people who acts one way at church and then goes around at school kind of embarrassed about my faith. I've just never been afraid to stand up for what I believe in.

My attitude is that whatever happens, I know God's behind me. He's got my back, and He is taking care of me. I know there are situations and groups of people in which being a Christian is not popular, and I realize there will be times I will not be accepted into cool things because of my beliefs. I'm okay with that. As long as I am true to God and true to myself, whether or not something is cool is really not important. I have set high standards for my life, and I hope you will do the same.

I've surrounded myself with friends who will help me be strong and uphold my standards, not people who will tempt me to do things I should not do. If you want to stay on the right path, having good friends around you is not optional; it's a must.

God knows that and loves me, and He loves you too. He took care of our imperfections by sending His Son to die on the cross. But as long as you are in this world as a Christian, situations will arise in which you can either take the easy way out and deny your faith, or you can stand up for your beliefs.

Even Peter denied Christ when times got tough (see Mark 14:66–72). If you have had times in your life when you have not stood up for your faith, don't let that get you down, just decide to start new and start standing up now. One of the best things about God is that you do not have to be perfect. God used imperfect people all the way through the Bible, people who did horrible things and made terrible mistakes. Yet God forgave them and still called them His disciples, His children, and He used them to further His Kingdom. If you follow Christ, decide today that you will do your "God thing" every chance you get, especially when it ends up surprising people.

> If you want to stay on the right path, having good friends around you is not optional; it's a must.

## TAKE A CHANCE

Different people in my family have said publicly many times that we will be fine if we lose everything we have gained as a result of *Duck Dynasty*. It's true. We were fine before we had a television show, and we will be fine when it's over. Some people are surprised to hear us say that. They think being a "celebrity" is the greatest thing ever and wonder how we could possibly think we will be okay when that changes. We'll be fine because we know who we are—apart from the things we get to do and enjoy because of *Duck Dynasty*. We are confident and secure in God and in ourselves. This is not because we are great people or anything. It's because we gave our lives to God, and our desire is to do His will, not our own. All of this is not an accident. We are intentional about giving our lives to God every day. We do not take our faith for granted.

Before our television show started, we went to God in prayer and asked Him to guide us in the decision whether or not to even do the show. We told Him that if it hurt our family in any way, then to take it away from us. We asked Him to keep us humble and keep our hearts turned toward Him and to be sure we do not get caught up in people's approval or in comparing ourselves to others. That is how we could walk away from it all and know we will be fine. We know God is with us, and every day, we try to love Him and love each other and live in ways that please Him. The great thing about this is that it gives us the freedom to take risks. Let me explain what I mean by that.

When you put your relationship with God first and you also have a great relationship with your family, you can risk having people get upset with you for standing up for your beliefs. You can risk being rejected because of your values, and you can even risk losing a boyfriend if the relationship is not going in a godly direction. You can risk looking or acting different from other people. You can do these things because you know you will be okay without them. You know God is with you and for you, and I hope you can also know your family is standing beside you. But even without your family's support, you can know that God is there. So many people are afraid of losing other people's approval that they do things that are not good for them—just to keep from being rejected. When you have God in your life, you are *never* rejected; you are always accepted and always loved.

If you know you need to take some kind of risk, then get your relationship with God strong and go for it. You will never know what you could have or experience in life unless you try. God made you an original. That means you are really special, and He has a really special plan for your life. You may have to risk something that currently feels secure in order to go after that plan, but with God's help, you may end up in an awesome situation if you'll just take the chance.

# GOD WANTS THE BEST

My mom talks to my siblings and me a lot about living a good life and having the courage to be ourselves. Both of our parents give us the room to be creative and to do different things, as long as we seek to please God and obey His Word. The reason they want us to obey His Word is that they know He wants the best for us. God tells us what to do and what not to do *not* so we will be bored or boring,

> The great thing about knowing God is with us is that it gives us the freedom to take risks.

but so we can live a good life on this earth. In His Word, He lays out a plan for us to be happy and content. And who doesn't want happiness and contentment?

Everything God tells us to do is for our good. He doesn't just make up arbitrary rules to see if we will obey them or not. He knows everything about us and everything about our lives, so centuries ago He wrote the Bible to give us a set of directions to follow if we want to live in strong, happy, peaceful ways. We get to choose whether to obey them or not.

One of the best things about God is that when we get off His path, He still loves us. He doesn't get angry with us or love us less. He loves us just the same, which is a lot more than we can ever wrap our minds around.

God wants the very best for you. That's what I want for you too. He made you an amazing person with all kinds of potential. I hope you'll live life His way, be an original, and express your uniqueness in every way you can, every chance you get.

# Live Original Challenge

*1.* How can you keep from falling into the trap of comparing yourself with others, so you can maximize your strong points and be okay with what you're not so good at?

_____

_____

_____

_____

_____

*2.* Do you try to see the best in other people and help them see what's good about themselves? How can you help someone around you learn to live original?

_____

_____

_____

_____

_____

*3.* What are some ways you can start living original right now? What things do you want to change about yourself: the way you look, the ways you spend your time, your values, or something else to better express who you really are?

_____

_____

_____

_____

_____

4. Based on what we've talked about in this book, what do you think God is calling you to do and be?

_____

_____

_____

_____

_____

## DON'T FORGET

**You're an original!
Find your uniqueness and express it every way you can.**

# A Quick Guide to Living Original

_I_ have written about a lot of things in this book. On the next couple of pages is a list of the key points of each chapter and the scriptures that encourage me as I try to do these things every day. I hope this will be a quick reminder of ways to be your best self and live original.

1. **Think happy, be happy:** "But may the righteous be glad and rejoice before God; may they be happy and joyful" (Psalm 68:3, NIV).

2. **Dream big:** " 'Anything is possible if a person believes' " (Mark 9:23).

3. **Never give up:** "We can rejoice, too, when we run into problems and trials, for we know that they help us develop endurance. And endurance develops strength of character, and character strengthens our confident hope of salvation" (Romans 5:3–4).

4. **Be confident:** "Do not throw away this confident trust in the Lord. Remember the great reward it brings you!" (Hebrews 10:35).

5. **Focus on fixing yourself:** "The temptations in your life are no different from what others experience. And God is faithful. He will not allow the temptation to be more than you can stand" (1 Corinthians 10:13).

6. **Let your smile change the world:** "In the same way, let your good deeds shine out for all to see, so that everyone will praise your heavenly Father" (Matthew 5:16).

7. **Commit acts of random kindness:** "For even the Son of Man came not to be served but to serve others and to give his life as a ransom for many" (Mark 10:45).

8. **Shake the hate:** " 'But to you who are willing to listen, I say, love your enemies! Do good to those who hate you. Bless those who curse you. Pray for those who hurt you' " (Luke 6:27–28).

9. **Remember that a friend's a friend forever:** "A friend loves at all times" (Proverbs 17:17, NIV).

10. **Respect relationships:** " 'Do to others whatever you would like them to do to you' " (Matthew 7:12).

11. **Don't let five seconds of awkward cause a lifetime of regret:** "Don't let anyone think less of you because you are young. Be an example to all believers in what you say, in the way you live, in your love, your faith, and your purity" (1 Timothy 4:12).

12. **Don't forget that stress causes a mess:** "Don't worry about tomorrow, for tomorrow will bring its own worries. Today's trouble is enough for today" (Matthew 6:34).

13. **Do something:** "What good is it, dear brothers and sisters, if you say you have faith but don't show it by your

actions? Can that kind of faith save anyone? Suppose you see a brother or sister who has no food or clothing, and you say, 'Good-bye and have a good day; stay warm and eat well'—but then you don't give that person any food or clothing. What good does that do? So you see, faith by itself isn't enough. Unless it produces good deeds, it is dead and useless" (James 2:14–17).

14. **Be the best you that you can be:** "You made all the delicate, inner parts of my body and knit me together in my mother's womb. Thank you for making me so wonderfully complex! Your workmanship is marvelous—how well I know it. You watched me as I was being formed in utter seclusion, as I was woven together in the dark of the womb. You saw me before I was born. Every day of my life was recorded in your book. Every moment was laid out before a single day had passed" (Psalm 139:13–16).

# Acknowledgments

**Mom and Dad:** I love you and thank you for all the ways you have taught me to love God and given me the freedom to live original. I can always count on your love and encouragement. As parents go, I'm feeling really blessed because you two are the best. Mom, thank you for all of your help with this project. You taught me everything I know, and I couldn't have done it without you.

**My amazing siblings:** Thank you so much for loving me and always being there for me. I'm blessed to be in the middle of this crazy family, and thankful to have brothers and sisters that are also my best friends. You make life fun!

**Philis Boultinghouse and the team at Howard Books:** Philis, you've been a wonderful friend to our family all of my life and I can't believe I'm actually working with you on my own book! To all the team at Howard Books, thanks for your creativity and commitment to making this great. You're the best!

**Mel Berger, Margaret Riley King, and John Howard (Two-Papa):** Thanks for guiding me through my first book publishing experience with such encouragement and enthusiasm. Two-Papa, thanks for giving me all of your wonderful and hilarious advice. You have set a great example of what living original is all about. Thank you for believing in me and in everything I do.

**Beth Clark:** Thank you for your amazing gift of putting my words on paper. Thank you for listening to my stories, and putting them perfectly in the book. From all the Robertsons, WE LOVE YOU!

# Notes

1 http://quoteinvestigator.com/2013/01/10/watch-your-thoughts.
2 http://thinkexist.com/quotation/watch_your_thoughts-they_be
come_your_words-watch/13673.html.
3 NIV.
4 http://www.joycemeyer.org/articles/ea.aspx?article=win_the
_battle_with_power_thoughts.
5 http://inventors.about.com/library/weekly/aa121997.htm.
6 http://www.brainyquote.com/quotes/authors/j/joe_namath
.html.
7 NIRV.
8 Van Moody, *The People Factor* (Nashville: Thomas Nelson Pub-
lishers, 2014), pp. xiii, xiv.
9 Ibid., p. xviii.
10 NIV.
11 NIV 2011.
12 http://www.mayoclinic.org/healthy-living/stress-management/in
-depth/stress-symptoms/art-20050987.
13 http://www.parenting.com/gallery/kids-who-make-difference?
page=2.
14 http://www.merriam-webster.com/dictionary/original.

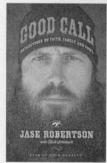

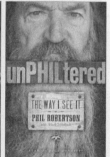